A Little Left of Center

C. L. GUSLER

A
Little
L e f T
of
Center

An Editor Reflects
on His Mennonite Experience

Daniel Hertzler

Foreword by Katie Funk Wiebe

DreamSeeker Books
TELFORD, PENNSYLVANIA

an imprint of
Pandora Press U.S.

Copublished with
Herald Press
Scottdale, Pennsylvania

Pandora Press U.S. orders, information, reprint permissions:
pandoraus@netreach.net
1-215-723-9125
126 Klingerman Road, Telford PA 18969
www.PandoraPressUS.com

Library of Congress Cataloguing-in-Publication Data
Hertzler, Daniel
    A little left of center : an editor reflects on his Mennonite
    experience / Daniel Herzler.
        p. cm.
    ISBN 0-9665021-7-5 (alk. paper)
        1. Hertzler, Daniel. 2. Editors—United States—Biography.
    3. Mennonites—United States—Biography. I. Title

BX8143.H47 A 3 2000
289.7'092—dc21'
[B]

00-043003

10 09 08 07 06 05 04 03 02 01 00   10 9 8 7 6 5 4 3 2 1

To Mary,
who put up with a lot

Contents

Foreword

My first contact with Dan Hertzler was in the early 1960s. I sent an article to *Christian Living* magazine. No answer. Months later came a check for $5 and some tattered remains. Editor Hertzler had chopped out the few sections he wanted to use and returned the rest. *So this is how editors work,* I surmised. But my next articles were published whole, and my relationship with Dan thereafter was always generous.

Although he is best known as an editor, Dan's wide-ranging ministry has included work as theologian, church leader, minister, Bible teacher, world traveler, and more. His ministry with Mennonite Publishing House (MPH) covered thirty-seven years, seventeen as *Gospel Herald* editor.

As his memoir shows, his Amish Mennonite origins were an unlikely heritage for his lengthy editing career. He could claim no ancestors as models. His call to MPH forced him to decide between becoming a farmer, a teacher, or an editor.

A privilege of retirement is to explain decisions from the perspective of age and greater wisdom. Education, Dan sees, has been an important lifelong quest. He never finished high school yet earned several bachelor's degrees as well as a Ph.D. and did post-graduate studies. Learning has been a goal in itself. He does admit to participating in one college "stunt."

Other factors that affected his development were his mother's early death and watching his father struggle to keep the family afloat. He saw his father as a man of principles.

Dan's ministry has been anchored in the Mennonite Church. Steadiness has marked his career. He knows the denominational shibboleths and loves the people. He has worked through many boundary-maintenance issues. Readers with similar backgrounds will resonate with his perplexities about the difference between recommendations and tests of fellowship, such as labeling paying honest debts a recomendation but not smoking cigarettes a test of fellowship.

Through his many years at MPH, Dan witnessed a more flexible approach to discipleship arise as Mennonite emphasis on rules eroded. He saw many changes in journalism, from shifts in printing technology to the emergence of editors with formal journalism training (not the case early in his career). Mennonite journalism standards rose under his leadership.

In this memoir Dan admits where he stands on certain issues like distinctive attire: "I have no great enthusiasm for it." He allows himself no self-justification for criticism of material he edited. His Amish Mennonite background has engrained in him not to push himself. Dan sees himself "a little left of center" for a Mennonite audience, especially on issues like behavior, church/state relations, violence, environmental concerns, and women's ministry. He has carried few flags; he admits he is more likely to report on than walk in a march.

As an editor Dan was forced to recognize how carefully readers peruse church publications and that some tolerate no departure from tradition. He and fellow editors wrestled with how to keep circulation up through interesting material—thus paying expenses—without compromising principles. Wryly he admits that "editorials, like sermons and the evening news, are eminently forgettable," yet he hopes his editorials may have moved readers along. This book will also move readers along in their understanding of Mennonite journalism.

—*Katie Funk Wiebe, Professor Emerita*
Tabor College, Hillsboro, Kansas

Author's Preface

I was an editor at Mennonite Publishing House for thirty-eight years. Right away I feel a need to qualify this statement. Those years included leaves of absence and so were not a solid block of editorial work. Also, some six months after I retired, I went back on staff part-time for three-and-a-half years and midway in this period received a forty-year award.

So there is a slight untidiness in speaking about my term of service as editor. But then editorial work itself was not tidy. Editors by definition are enthusiasts for the subjects treated in their publications. On occasion they may be more enthusiastic than their readers. Indeed an editor is in some sense an educator, and educators are never satisfied. So editors may tend to push their readers and some will be uncomfortable.

I was dismayed by a reference to Mennonite Publishing House that once appeared in a Mennonite district conference publication. "Materials coming out of Scottdale," this writer said, "are generally a little left of center." I was concerned because I disliked the burden of a stereotype. I had hoped to be able to describe and report on things as they really are—to break down stereotypes. The writer had stereotyped me.

On further thought I was inclined to accept his stereotype. At least he had not labeled us reactionary. And it occurred to me that the work of an editor for a Christian publication might well take him "a little left of center" if the center represents the status quo. Should not an editor be an advocate for change?

Because the church supported me for over four decades, I owe it some account of how I became an editor and what I think I did. This book tells that story. Although I did not often have time to reflect on it, to be supported by the church is not a role to accept lightly. I hope I did not do so.

I begin with the story of my family background. I could start otherwise for the church itself is a family. Indeed the amount of detail available on my family used to embarrass me, since some lack this luxury. Then came Alex Haley's *Roots* and it seemed genealogy was an "in" topic. If a descendant of slaves could find and rejoice in his family tree, why not the rest of us? Of course to write a memoir has its own hazards. Now my friends—and any enemies—can say to themselves about me, "Now I understand why he is the way he is."

I find as I reflect another reason to write. There are things I want to say and I feel more comfortable saying them as part of my story than getting up on a stump and "preaching." So here is what I have found as I reflected on—and in some cases did research on—my background and my experiences.

This account has the memoir's limitations. This is how I saw matters. Others looking from other perspectives no doubt saw things differently. I have tried to allow for that. I also find that most of my work was probably not very far "left of center"—just enough to cause an occasional disturbance.

As I review these materials I see the usual tension between a chronological and a thematic approach. Unless one is to write only a diary or a strict chronology, one finds oneself carrying some themes through to the end before going on with the rest of the story. I think there are enough reference points to keep you from getting confused about this, but be forewarned.

—*Daniel Hertzler*
Scottdale, Pennsylvania

A
Little
Left
of
Center

1

Born and Bred on the Watershed

The farm in Southern Berks County, Pennsylvania, where I was born and raised is situated at the watershed of two river systems. Most of the land drains to the east toward the Delaware River and the Delaware Bay. One corner of the field drains west toward the Susquehanna River and the Chesapeake Bay.

Does the place one has come from affect the person one becomes? Which is more important, nature or nurture? As I reflect on the story of my life I find it of some interest to recall that I have on more than one occasion been on the border between two systems. Perhaps some experiences in my place of origin helped to prepare me for later efforts to serve as interpreter between scholars and laity, as moderator between conservatives and liberals. Generally I was in the middle, but usually a little to the left.

I have at times been attracted to radical positions, but generally found them more interesting to read about than to practice. As a boy I read with pleasure the adventures of Robin Hood and his merry men who lived in the forest, stole the king's deer and drank "nut brown ale." But that was as far as it went. I have been attracted by the idea of intentional community but have always ended up paying my own bills instead of pooling incomes and expenses.

I was a child of the Great Depression. Like my birth on a watershed, this had educational significance. However, I do not remember being oppressed in the same way as my wife Mary, who grew up on a farm in Ohio. Her father was in partnership with her grandfather who lost money in a bank that failed. She was not allowed to drink all the milk she wanted because milk had to be sold. I cannot recall ever being denied any basic food.

Not that there was much for us in the way of frills, but we were able to persevere because our farm was in many respects a self-contained unit. All meat, milk, eggs, and vegetables were produced at home. Unwrapped bread could be bought for five cents a loaf—delivered!—and other necessities came from Stiteler's store in Elverson. Grocery bills were modest.

Someone had named the farm "Summit Level," although only a little more than an area for the buildings was level. There was a pond on the other side of the road. It was drained by a brook that ran through pasture fields and provided some entertainment for small children with homemade fishing rods.

Reports had it that the farm once had certain features of affluence, such as a pond on the back lawn. By the time I knew it, the area of the pond had become devoted to a more pragmatic purpose as a pig pen. I heard also that the lingering signs of ostentation were based on farm prosperity from the Civil War, possibly related to inflation in the price of wheat.

This was the place my father, Melvin, moved to in 1921 with his parents, Levi and Katherine, and his younger brother Milford. There he brought my mother after their marriage in December 1924. She was Susan Shenk, a daughter of Daniel Shenk, a minister in the Mennonite community at Denbigh, Virginia, where Dad went after his year at Goshen College. To live for a time at Denbigh was a life-changing experience for him.

In 1994 my brother Truman and I went to visit John Stoltzfus, a cousin of our father, to ask him what he remembered about Dad and Uncle Milford. The only specific thing he recalled for us was that in Tennessee they were "sharp dressers." This was of interest since when I knew Dad he did not pay much attention to high quality apparel. However, he did keep his collars closed, even on work shirts. And I never saw him in short sleeves. There are pictures of him as a young adult that support John's observation. How he got from one style to the other is accounted for by his encounter with Bishop George R. Brunk in Denbigh, Virginia.

The bishop was concerned with what sociologists would refer to as "boundary maintenance" and would approach young men new in the community to address them on the issue of clothing. Dad and several others were accosted by the bishop and the experience, he told me years later, left him deflated. So he took off his neckties and began to wear a "plain" coat. But he kept the ties and took them along to Pennsylvania where we children once found them and began to model them. Our mother was not pleased with this and the ties disappeared.

A related characteristic of Dad's that was evidently modified by this experience was his penchant for clowning and practical jokes. Uncle Milford said that as a schoolboy in Tennessee, Dad and a buddy climbed the bell tower and to hold the rope so the teacher's assistant could not ring the bell. I also heard a story from someone of how as a young adult in Denbigh he and an accomplice who were not invited to a wedding reception turned out the lights and made off with the wedding cake. I believe the sound of the car was identified and so they were able to pursue them and retrieve the cake.

This sort of playfulness seems to have been driven out of him by the encounter with the bishop. However a glimmer of it lived on in his tendency toward self-deprecating humor. I was told that as a guest teacher of a Sunday school class he convulsed the group by an offhand reference to his tractor. He was discussing a passage of Scripture that calls for generosity and confessed his own hesitance. A neighbor wanted to borrow his tractor, he told them, and he did not want to loan it. "Of course," he said, "the tractor was no good." It struck them funny.

In a time when many of us in the Mennonite Church have concluded that wearing peculiar clothing is not the place to take our stand, it is hard to know exactly how to evaluate an experience like his. Was my father's personality violated? The best I can do is note that adopting plain clothing likely helped open the way for Dad to marry the minister's daughter. It also prepared him for entry into the Amish Mennonite community at Morgantown, Pennsylvania, where plain clothing was expected.

In contrast to this, Uncle Milford told about the experience of his cousin John Stoltzfus (he whom we later interviewed) when he moved to Pennsylvania. He reported that John spoke to the deacon of the Conestoga Mennonite Church about membership in the congregation. The deacon said he would need to wear a plain coat, so John joined another denomination. Today this congregation would receive such a person gladly.

Susan Shenk was the fifth child and second daughter of Daniel and Matilda Hilty Shenk. Matilda was Daniel's second wife. His first wife, Rachel Stemen, had died in 1890 (probably from tuberculosis) and he remarried in 1891. Altogether Daniel would have fourteen children, five with his first wife and nine with his second. When Susie was two years old her father was called from Ohio to Denbigh to serve as an associate with Isaac Hertzler as a minister in the Warwick River congregation.[1] There were to be two more sisters. The four were Elizabeth, the oldest of the four, Susie, Alice and Mayme.

Alice would marry J. Paul Sauder, a high school teacher from New Holland, Pennsylvania. Their twin sons, Joseph and John, were roughly two years younger than I, about the same age as my sister Katherine. It was a great occasion when Uncle Paul's family came to visit. But in the mid-1930s, the Eastern

Mennonite Board of Missions sent the Sauders to Tampa, Florida, as church planters, and we could not get together as often.

About this same time, Mayme married Joseph Longacher, a builder in the Denbigh community. Their home became a place to visit in later years.

Elizabeth never married but became an entrepreneur who sold home baked cakes at the Farmers' Market in Newport News. Leftover cakes were served in the Shenk household. Dad remarked on one occasion that the men of the household did not seem hungry. Evidently they were full of cake.

During one visit to Grandpa Shenks', Aunt Elizabeth said she wanted to treat us children, so she bought us ice cream sodas. We had never before encountered soda pop and the bite was almost more than we could handle. I am sure she was puzzled by our lack of enthusiasm for her treat.

This was a Mennonite, not an Amish Mennonite family as my father's was. My grandmother's parents were David Hilty and Elizabeth Thut and my grandfather's were Henry Shenk and Susanna Brenneman. All of these family lines ultimately trace back to Switzerland where they were members of the group which Evelyn King Mumaw has characterized as the "hated, hunted, persecuted Anabaptists."[2]

David Hilty was a Mennonite bishop in Nampa, Idaho, who died of apoplexy in 1914 at age sixty-nine. His obituary reports that "On Saturday morning he went about his work as usual. About 11:00 a.m. he went to a sick neighbor nearby to help with some chores. Then he came home, sat down to the dinner table with the *Herald* which the mail had just brought and while eating and reading, dropped over without a moment's warning."[3]

Henry and Susanna Shenk had four sons who grew to adulthood. All were called to church leadership: two as bishops, one (my grandfather) as a minister, and the fourth as a deacon. As recounted by Mumaw, the leadership connection had an influence on Susanna. She smoked a pipe, evidently a common practice among her peers. "In those days we thought those things were good for us," says Mumaw in a monologue on the life of Susanna. But with four sons in the ministry the pipe smoking became an issue. When pressure against it began to build, she and her sister would meet to smoke in the outhouse. Finally, according to the tradition, while visiting her family at Denbigh, she walked to the Warwick River and threw the pipe as far as she could out into the river.

Susanna's family had moved to Ohio from Pennsylvania by way of the Shenandoah Valley of Virginia. It is reported that in Pennsylvania the children of Melchior Brenneman, her pioneer ancestor, had played with Indian children of the Conestoga tribe, who "lived peaceably with the Mennonite folk for many years." Then they "were barbarously murdered in the year 1763 by a gang of fiends who have gone down in Pennsylvania history under the opprobrious name of 'The Paxtang Boys.'"[4]

I never got to know Grandpa Shenk well. He was over seventy when I was born and lived more than 300 miles away. I remember him as an old man with a white beard who sat at the head of the table and who said "thar" when most other people said "there."

I do vaguely recall one personal interaction with him. As I remember it, sometime in the late 1930s our family was visiting in his home and we children found some toys which we assumed were for us. So I took it on myself to thank him. He seemed unhappy with my response. The ambiguity of the situation made me uncomfortable. I do not recall what happened to the toys.

Grandpa's youngest son John has written of him, "Papa's expression was grave and his movements deliberate. His speech was precise and proper, giving evidence of the school teacher in him." He notes further that "I experienced my father as a very serious, sometimes melancholy person. He seldom smiled.

I wish our relationship had been closer. No doubt the fifty-seven year difference in our ages contributed to a lack of emotional closeness. I think also he was somewhat inhibited in any expression of emotion."[5]

Yet he is remembered as an effective pastor and preacher. Sometime after his ordination to the ministry in 1900, he stopped teaching school and supported himself by farming alone to have more time for the ministry although "his success as a farmer was limited."[6] Late in life he passed out while preaching a sermon. "He was carried outside. A little later the people were shocked to see him walk back in. He announced to the congregation, 'There is something more I want to say.'"[7]

I think my father was rather awed by his father-in-law. In part it may have been the precise and proper aspect of his personality and manner of working since energy was more apparent in my father's style than precision. Late in his life he wrote to me that "Grandpa was careful with his words. He said some men 'paint' and some 'slap it on.'"

My parents were in no hurry to get married. If we may assume that they were committed to each other when Dad left for Pennsylvania in the spring of 1921, they would have corresponded for more than three-and-a-half years until their marriage on December 10, 1924. We children once stumbled on a cache of Dad's letters in the attic. I recall that one of them began, "The top o' the morning to ye, Susie M' dear." I don't remember having read much farther. Maybe it seemed too much like invading sacred territory.

I do not know why it took so long to prepare for the wedding. Maybe they felt they couldn't afford it sooner. Since Grandpa Hertzler had foregone his pension, the farm had to support a couple of retirement age plus two young adults. The size of the operation was expanded from what it was at Denbigh where a sale bill dated March 14, 1921, lists only two mules and five cows—along with the basic items of farm machinery. Details of their financial management at this point were not reported to me although Dad spoke with some satisfaction about the herd of Holstein cows they bought in Susquehana County, Pennsylvania.

One thing my mother did during the interim was to attend one year at the newly established Eastern Mennonite School near Harrisonburg, Virginia. She enrolled in the Elementary Bible Course during the 1922-1923 school year. I received a transcript of her credits and found that her grades ranged from 88 in "Gospels" to 97 in "Music II." [8]

When they finally married, Dad was thirty and she was twenty-six. He brought her to a double farm house where his parents and his younger brother Milford lived on one side and he and his bride on the other. Between the two was a hall with an open stairway leading to the second floor. (The stairway had a banister which small children found useful for sliding down.) Here I was born on October 19, 1925, two days after my mother's twenty-seventh birthday. Dad once remarked that she "almost gave herself a birthday present."

There were to be six children in our family, four of whom have lived to maturity. My birth was to be followed by my sister Katherine's on April 22, 1928, and my brother Truman's on F.D. Roosevelt's birthday—January 30, 1930. Paul came along on September 8, 1931 and Martha Carol, December 15, 1933, (I was allowed to help name her and I chose "Carol" because of the proximity to Christmas.)

Paul died before his third birthday from an overdose of chocolate-covered medication he and Truman discovered when put to bed for an afternoon nap. There was to be one more girl, a premature infant who died just after my mother on May 6, 1935. Today Mother and baby would likely survive. Pneumonia took my mother. Sulfa drugs became available about five years later.[9]

What do I remember from growing up on a southeastern Pennsylvania farm? Of course I recall my parents, since to a small child parents are the most impressive part of the world.

As I reflect on these early experiences, numbers of them seem to involve an exchange of power. In some cases I won; in others I lost; in some there was compromise and even cooperation.

I remember a conflict over afternoon naps. "I can't sleep!" I protested. Mamma finally gave in and allowed me to skip the naps. Another problem was woolen underwear. Evidently Pennsylvania winters much impressed my mother, who was from Virginia. She prescribed woolen underwear, and I complained that it scratched. So she devised little vests of some unscratchy material. But I was never really satisfied until I was allowed to wear cotton underwear.

A test of power which I lost involved a childhood expression of frustration. On one occasion I responded directly to my mother, "Oh Mamma you're awful!" She did not take this lightly, nor did my father. He later took me to the wood shed and whipped me. It is the only recollection I have of being whipped.

Another obvious occasion where I lost occurred after we were forbidden to swing on the back yard gate. I did it anyhow, fell off, and broke my right arm. Dr. Mengel set it in our living room, and I recall the setting as a singularly painful experience. For six weeks I was denied the effective use of the arm. When the splint finally came off I found I was out of the habit of using the arm.

More pleasant is the memory of how my mother used to call me in the morning. At this point in my experience the bedroom where I slept was directly above the kitchen. To call me, Mamma would tap on the ceiling with a broom handle and I would respond by thumping a foot on the floor. The novelty of this method appealed to me.

Literature for children was not plentiful in our home, but I recall several books, two of them religious and one literary. One was called *First Steps for Little Feet,* of which all I can remember is the title. Another was *A Hive of Busy Bees,* which seems to have been an effort to provide moral guidance for children with stories illustrating "Be this" and "Be that." Then there was *A Child's Garden of Verses,* by Robert Louis Stevenson who had died in 1894, the year my father was born. It is a classic and I am confident it is still in print after more than 100 years. Numbers of its descriptions of a child's experience remain in my mind.

My own early experiences included play—and before long—work. Play was abetted by a pretty good sled that made me stand out at the one room school where sleds were in short supply. But toys became scarce in the Great Depression. I recall being impressed by a pound of hard candy for a Christmas present. One year Truman and I received stuffed animals. His was a rabbit and mine an elephant, and I was old enough that a stuffed elephant didn't impress me. Truman and I got into a squabble, and he grabbed my elephant by the trunk and tore it under the chin. Someone repaired it, but the elephant was never the same again.

Work came early. My baby book notes that "at two and a half, he tried to chop wood and before he was four brought in the cows." But the first work I remember was carrying wood for the kitchen range. To a small boy that wood box seemed enormous! I would rather feed grain to the cows. The time came when I was old enough to feed cows and before I left the farm I had more experience feeding cows than I cared for.

In summer 1934 I sidestepped a work assignment and the result was a family tragedy. No one has ever held me responsible for this, but the experience is filed in my memory bank and perhaps it serves as a comment on the question of how much responsibility should be expected of an eight year old.

I was assigned to lie down with Truman and Paul, ages four and two, until they went to sleep for an afternoon nap. One day I slipped out of the house after the noon meal in time to avoid this chore. Instead of coming after me, Mamma put the boys to bed by themselves. They got into some chocolate-covered laxative tablets and Paul ate too many. Ida Kurtz Glick, a teenage mother's helper in our home at that time, remembers that she checked the contents of the pills and found they included belladonna and strychnine. Efforts to induce vomiting worked with Truman but, as she recalls, "little Paul soon went into convulsions." An ambulance took him to the hospital where they pumped his stomach, but it was too late.

Less than a year later, in spring 1935, my mother died. Some events from the day of her death are engraved on my mind. I had not been called in the usual manner and had to get myself up that morning. When I got downstairs there was stale smoke in the kitchen. Evidently someone had fired the stove improperly. The smell of smoke was depressing. Also a black wreath hung on the front door. Katherine and I suggested to each other that this must mean that someone was ill in our house. But I think we knew in our hearts that our mother had died.

Later we went to breakfast on Grandmother's side of the house and my father's eyes were red from weeping. I had never seen my father cry, so this was a strange experience. Then came the funeral, which was an awkward event for a nine-year-old boy. Attending were some younger cousins who began to play with my brother Truman. But I was old enough to realize that I should not play at my mother's funeral.

The attention our family received was embarrassing to me. It was as if we were put on display. Later came men from the Mennonite community to help with the farm work. This too embarrassed me, since it demonstrated that Dad was not fully able to take care of his responsibilities.

My mother's obituary in the *Gospel Herald* filled in some details I would not have known. It reported that before her marriage she "did nursing." I do not have the impression that she was trained as a nurse, but I suppose she would have provided general care for the sick, or more likely, assisted mothers and new babies.

The obituary also noted that she taught Sunday school and she gave the first dollar toward the beginning of a "mission" in Newport News. I presume this is now the Huntington Mennonite Church. "Her greatest pleasure was to be able to do something for her family, especially teaching the Bible to her children." Her ability in music was also mentioned, a skill passed on to three of my siblings but not to me.[10]

Two funerals in less than a year added to the usual financial strain of the Depression. As a result Dad was delayed in buying grave stones. He finally buried field stones in the cemetery at the Conestoga Mennonite Church west of Morgantown so he could be sure to locate the plots when he could afford grave stones.

Dad never remarried. It was as if he had loved once and never again. I think also he had a sense of personal pride and perhaps observed that he did not have much to offer a new wife. He was a poor farmer with four small children. But he was determined to keep the family together, so he hired housekeepers. The first one, Mary Yoder, stayed two years. After her came Kathryn Mast, who remained until his death in 1964 and was included in his will as part of the family.

In his prime Dad was a tireless worker. I doubt either Truman or I was ever able to match him. But truly effective farm management eluded him. From the time they moved to Pennsylvania until 1934 he was teamed with Uncle Milford, who could not work as vigorously as he but was more adept at long-range planning.

Sometime in the early 1930s Dad broke his right arm cranking the Fordson tractor. I recall he was still able to drive the old Dodge by reaching through the steering wheel to shift gears with his left hand. (I did the same thing myself when I broke a finger in 1979.) But he could not milk for some six weeks, and Uncle Milford used this as an occasion to get a milking machine. To run the vacuum pump for the milker they bought a used Delco power unit.

These had been developed to generate electricity in rural areas where power lines were not yet available. Since the batteries with this one were old and worn, the only light they produced was in the barn while the unit was running. So we had electric lights in the barn during the milking but only oil lamps in the house.

Uncle Milford had a solution for this problem also. There was a small dam on the farm. He arranged to have a generator placed in an old mill below the dam with a water wheel to turn it. The house was wired and a line run from the old mill to the farm buildings. But the flow of water was not adequate to produce power on a regular basis. So the project failed, but the house was wired and waiting when we got connected to an electric power line in 1937.

When Uncle Milford moved in 1934 his farm was only two miles away. He and Dad shared some equipment and co-operated in farm work. For the first six years they owned a tractor jointly and as long as grain was threshed they did this together. Also after my mother died I recall that we went to their place for Sunday dinner week after week. The quality of Aunt Martha's cooking was high on the scale.

The extended family thus provided its own sort of support to us. As long as my grandmother lived—nine years after my mother's death—this was the family homestead and the place for family buffet dinners that had a special appeal to a growing boy. There was also the opportunity to listen to men's after dinner talk.

Growing up without a mother was sometimes awkward, although we were basically well cared for. Occasionally I observed other boys with their mothers and got a glimpse of what I was missing. But I took grim satisfaction from the fact that no one was telling me to keep my feet dry.

2

The Blessing and Burden of Family History

If I am left of center, are there clues to be found in the account of my Hertzler family background? Of course, Mennonite theology and practices are viewed by many as radical. In certain respects, the Amish are more radical than Mennonites. By declining to purchase electricity or automobiles and refusing to install telephones they subvert the dominant paradigm in significant ways.

My community had been marginal from its beginning in North America. Not only were my ancestors among the Germans invited to the English colony of Pennsylvania by the Penn family. They were also in the Anabaptist tradition and, within that heritage, among the Amish who had split from the Mennonites in Switzerland in 1693-1697, some ten years after the first permanent Mennonite settlement in North America at Germantown in 1683.

So Jacob Hertzler, my ancestor and the first Amish bishop in Pennsylvania, was a marginal person when on September 9, 1749 he reached Philadelphia.. The Mennonite communities which were to become Franconia and Lancaster Mennonite Conferences were already well on the way, but the Amish did not join these.

Instead Jacob moved to an area near Hamburg, north of the Mennonites and between them. The three settlements form a triangle with Skippack and Lancaster at the base and Hamburg at the point. *The Hertzler-Hartzler Family History* reports that on arrival Jacob "moved at once to the vicinity of Hamburg where he became the minister and bishop for the Amish settlers." He also served a congregation at Malvern, about sixty miles south, and organized the Conestoga Amish Mennonite Church near Morgantown, about midway between the two. "One word of mouth account says he walked the sixty miles from Hamburg to Malvern in two days."[11]

Jacob Hertzler is buried in a small cemetery on the Hertzler farm some two miles west of Hamburg, Pennsylvania. In 1901 a granite memorial was placed over the grave. My daughter-in-law, Laurel Schmidt Hertzler, made a rubbing of the message. I have the framed copy in my study. It reads, "Jacob Hertzler. Pioneer settler. Preacher of the gospel. Born in Switzerland—1703—came to America—1749, died—1786. First wife died in Europe, second wife Catherine Ruegy, and second son Jacob buried here."

From here on the family trail is less distinct for several generations. We learn that Jacob had three sons and a daughter. In order they were John, Jacob, Fannie, and Christian. Of Fannie it is said that she married John Kauffman. "The family moved from Upper Berne Township, Berks Co., Pa., to Somerset County, Pa. Later they moved to the rural area near Dayton, Ohio. No further records of their whereabouts is available. There were two sons and four daughters."[12] The rest of *The Hertzler-Hartzler Family History* is given to Jacob's three sons and their descendants.

My own family line comes from Christian, the youngest son who married Barbara Yoder. Then in turn had a son Christian who married Nancy Zug. Then there was Isaac, who married Mary Kanagy and my grandfather, Levi, who married Katherine Stoltzfus.

At this point I begin to have personal memories. I have also seen the graves of Isaac and Mary near Elverson and I have in my possession a desk which is said to have belonged to them. An antique of documented value! I got this in 1977 from my uncle Milford Hertzler who had inherited it in 1944 from his parents' estate. Yet Isaac Hertzler's 1891 will designated it for his son Joseph, my grandfather's oldest brother.[13] How it came into our family is a mystery.

My cousin, the late Beatrice Hershey Hallman, once re-marked that Great Grandma Mary was a melancholy person. I never thought to ask her how she knew this and what other information about the family she could supply. Now it is too late.

Grandpa himself never told me this or any other stories since our lives overlapped only briefly. I was born on October 19, 1925, in the old farmhouse in eastern Pennsylvania where Grandpa lived the last six years of his life. I believe someone said that as a small child I used to follow him around. I do not remember this, but I have one vague memory of being held on his lap. This serves as a check on the beginning of my memories since he died at the age of seventy-seven, two months after my second birthday. His death is noted in my baby book: "Dec. nineteenth he lost his Grandpa Hertzler with whom he was quite chummy." I think we both could have enjoyed a longer relationship. His family was scattered about and I was probably the first grandchild that he was able to see on a regular basis.

I remember Grandma Katherine better, since she lived an-other seventeen years. She was a small round faced woman, friendly but not effusive. She never told me many stories ei-ther although she could have had plenty to tell. Some can be pieced together from the record.

The community where Jacob Hertzler settled was on the frontier, and Silas Hertzler observes that this congregation suf-fered Indian violence. He suggests this may be the reason there is no Mennonite church in that area today. J. Lemar and Lois Ann Mast write that members of the Amish community west of Hamburg were invited to relocate by Jacob Morgan, a provincial army captain during the French and Indian War. "Morgan invited them to the rich farmland in southern Berks County where he was living. It was through Morgan's influence that the Conestoga Amish Mennonite community began."[14] This community has survived, whereas the Hamburg and Malvern Amish communities died out.

Isaac Hertzler moved from Morgantown to Long Green, Maryland in 1849. The Long Green Amish community lasted only about a generation, although a cemetery there is still maintained by an organization that holds a meeting once a year in a nearby Church of the Brethren meetinghouse. But here my Grandfather Levi was born in 1850, and from here he went out to find his place in life.

As reported by my Uncle Milford Hertzler, he found a place he liked at Topeka, Indiana, and the girl he liked was Katherine Stoltzfus at Concord, Tennessee. Her parents objected to moving her to Indiana (she was only nineteen at the time of their marriage) so the couple settled in Tennessee. One remark I remember my grandmother making was that she considered herself to have been too young when she married. Her six children must have gotten the message. Only one was married before age thirty!

The children were born in two groups: two girls, Mae and Ida, and two boys, Isaac Truman and John Eugene, within seven years. Then my father Melvin came ten years later and Milford, the youngest, after another three years. (The two oldest sons carried traditional Hertzler names, Isaac and John, but in my experience did not use them, preferring their middle names.)

How Grandma Katherine got to Tennessee is described by Paton Yoder in his book on her grandfather, Tennessee John Stoltzfus.[15] Tennessee John led a family group from eastern Lancaster County, Pennsylvania, to Knox County, Tennessee in 1872. Included was my grandmother, a fourteen-year-old.

: community that developed was somewhat frail, and when she and Levi married she was not yet of age. Both could be reasons why her parents wanted to keep her nearby.

The family in which Grandma had grown up would not be described as "typically Amish." When she was a small child, her father John S. Stoltzfus was banned by his Amish community for participating in the underground railroad and campaigning for Abraham Lincoln. As Yoder reports, "The ban meant almost complete isolation from wife and family and from members of his congregation." Yoder observes, for example, that there were no more children, although his wife was only thirty-four at the probable time of the ban. The result of this church discipline seems to have been to drive John S. to heavy drinking, so that the family finances went downhill. Another pressure on John reported by Yoder was that a substitute he had hired to take his place in the Union army during the Civil War was killed and the man's coat was sent to him.[16]

Finally after perhaps a dozen years John S. went along with the family to Tennessee and "made his peace, the ban was removed, either by formal or informal process, domestic relations were resumed, and John S. is spoken of with great respect by his descendants." But he remained a colorful character, as illustrated by the following anecdote. A communion sermon at the church in Tennessee with visiting ministers from the North went longer than John thought was necessary. So he got up, took his hat from the hook, and walked out muttering, "If you are going to talk the whole day, I'm going home."[17]

Life in Tennessee was not easy for my grandparents. As recounted by Uncle Milford in a 1981 interview I had with him, it seems to have taken Grandpa more than twenty-five years to find employment in line with his skills. He tried farming as well as operating a sawmill in partnership with his wife's uncle, John B. Stoltzfus.[18] Also for a time he bought and sold market items. The family situation was made more difficult by a fire that occurred a few years after their marriage. The house and its contents burned. All that was saved was one small piece of furniture. As Uncle Milford put it, "All their wedding things were lost and my mother said later that you never recover from a fire."

Finally in 1900 at age fifty Grandpa became a U.S. mail carrier. This work seemed to fit him well. Uncle Milford, who was three in 1900, remembers that "at 8:00 p.m. he would start for the bedroom winding his alarm clock because he had to get up at 4:00 or 5:00 a.m. to go to the post office, an hour's drive. Then he would stop at the house about 9:00 a.m. to change horses and eat a lunch. His route was about 24 miles and took most of the day."

Grandma had an unmarried brother named Christian who took it upon himself to manage a $1,000 inheritance she received from her parents' estate. I got to know Uncle Crist a little as I was growing up. He lived on a farm about five miles from ours where he died in the late thirties. He had no will, and my father drew the assignment to administer the estate on behalf of Uncle Crist's younger sister Elizabeth who had lived with him. I remember that Dad found this task a legal drudgery.

I don't recall that Dad ever mentioned how Uncle Crist had affected his destiny—and mine—but Uncle Milford filled me in on this during our 1981 conversation. Evidently there were three unmarried adult children living at home when their parents died and the household was disbanded. Uncle Milford did not date this event, but Yoder reports that Elizabeth died in 1899, so it must have been about that time.[19] The two girls, Mary and Lizzie, found employment in Goshen, Indiana, and "Uncle Crist went roving."

He first moved to Oscoda County, Michigan, and reported that this was the place for others to come. Grandma invested her $1,000 there. Grandpa and Grandma were preparing to move, but then Uncle Crist decided the winters were too cold.

So he moved to Texas and Grandma recovered her $1,000 and sent it to Texas. But before they could move there was a flood and this was not the place to go. The $1,000 was transferred to a rooming house in Knoxville, Tennessee. Then word came of land available at Denbigh, Virginia, near a Mennonite colony of which Grandpa's youngest brother Isaac was one of the founders.

So in the spring 1917 Uncle Milford moved to Virginia, where Uncle Crist had already gone. My father was at Goshen College that year and after college he moved there too. In 1918 the parents moved to Denbigh forgoing the pension my grandfather would have received by carrying mail a little longer. But by then Uncle Crist had heard of land in Pennsylvania. So in 1921 my grandparents and their two unmarried sons moved to Berks County, Pennsylvania.

Thus within a period of seventy-two years my grandfather had closed the loop opened when his father moved to Long Green, Maryland, in 1849, a year before Grandpa was born. He returned in time to be buried six years later in the cemetery where his parents had been buried after retiring in the community they had left. He financed the farm with money borrowed from the Hertzlers whose family had stayed at home instead of migrating from place to place as his family had done. The farm was not in the Conestoga Valley, the heart of the Amish Mennonite settlement, but it was close enough for the family to be involved.

The Denbigh interlude was more significant to our family than its three-year duration might imply. However, Uncle Milford remembered that his oldest sister Mae had been against the move because of the presence there of George R. Brunk, a conservative and authoritarian Mennonite bishop. "But my parents got along all right there," said Uncle Milford. "My father had his coat changed and taught a men's class. My mother did not wear a 'cape' dress, but she still was asked to teach a women's class."

For more than a century developing Amish and progressive Mennonites have been interacting and melding in North America. In both groups there have been Old Orders who say "no" to specific changes while many adapt to aspects of the wider culture. As these groups found each other and sought to work together, some have observed a characteristic difference in polity: those in the Amish tradition have been seen as more "congregational" while Mennonites have tended to see authority vested in a wider "conference" structure.

These different assumptions have been subtle but at times sources of tension, as Yoder observes in telling of the Concord, Tennessee, Amish Mennonite community. When Tennessee John Stoltzfus died in 1887, the congregation he had led was left with no one in charge. Two other ministers had left before: Joseph Detweiler had moved to Ohio and John's own son John B. had joined the Plymouth Brethren. But within months H. H. Good, a minister from Allen County, Ohio, came to visit, and the next year he returned to become the leader of the congregation.

Yoder reports that Good represented a new background for the Concord congregation. The previous ministers had been Amish Mennonite but Good was Mennonite. There were roughly equal numbers of Mennonites and Amish Mennonites in the area and Good was able to unite the two groups and to affiliate with the Virginia Mennonite Conference. On April 6, 1889, twenty-six charter members from both groups made up the reorganized congregation. A new meetinghouse was erected in 1897. Pastor Good served until 1904, when he resigned due to his own ill health and discord in the congregation.[20]

My aunt, Mae Hertzler Hershey, felt the decline in the congregation was related to differences between Mennonites and Amish Mennonites. "Some who were Amish always stayed Amish in their ideas," she wrote in 1953. "One 'bone of contention' was that of joining a conference. The Amish are congregational in government. If the congregation belongs to a conference, then conference rules." She reported that at the time of her writing only three of the original families remained in the area.[21]

Economic factors also had an effect. My father once commented that when he was growing up people said, "Get out of here if you can." Nevertheless, there is still a Mennonite congregation at Concord.

In the fall of 1993, my wife Mary and I were vacationing in Tennessee and stopped to view the meetinghouse and graveyard. The site was hard pressed by the clutter of urbanization, but the building was in good repair and the cemetery showed recent burials, a sort of negative sign of congregational life. The 1995 *Mennonite Yearbook* reported twenty-six members and the pastor's name, Matt Matteson.

There may be none of the original families in the church today, but I consider it more important to know that the church is there. Family and church are interrelated but not identical. They need to support each other, but in this neither is completely successful.

Of the six children in my grandfather's family, five are listed in *The Hertzler-Hartzler Family History* as "Mennonite." Uncle Eugene is listed as simply "Farmer." I asked Uncle Milford how it was that Uncle Eugene had become estranged from the church. His recollection was that he had been baptized while working in Illinois but later neglected the church. He married a Tennessee girl his mother did not want him to marry and later "when they came to Pennsylvania our church was so conservative you couldn't see anybody from the outside joining it." When I knew him Uncle Gene seemed to have made peace with his mother for I sensed in them mutual respect. But he declined to participate in church—although his wife and daughters joined the local Evangelical Church.

At the end of our interview Uncle Milford ruminated about evangelism. He said, "I am sorry we were not very evangelistic in Tennessee. A few people came to our church and some others liked us. But we weren't good at bringing them in."

Maybe Uncle Milford was too hard on himself. They were, after all, Yankee Amish speaking Pennsylvania Dutch. Perhaps in another generation or two they would have learned the local lingo as well as more about how to make the gospel of peace attractive. A task that all Mennonite congregations find to be a challenge. And yes, Uncle Milford, there is a Mennonite church at Concord even if it may not include any of the original families.

3

Life With Father

My earliest memory of my father Melvin is of his coming in from the barn at my bedtime. The memory is symbolic. From the time he moved to Pennsylvania in 1921 until his death in 1964, a large part of his personal agenda was spelled WORK. He told me once that in the early days he thought work was enough. Then it was called to his attention that there was more to life than work, and he sought to take the broader dimensions of life more seriously.

One way this was impressed on him was through the traditional holidays of the Amish Mennonite community. We were expected to fast and rest on Good Friday and to go to church on Ascension Day for the preaching marathon. Some took Good Friday as an occasion for friendly visits to others of the community. Dad told me that early in his Pennsylvania experience one of the brothers of the church came to call on him on Good Friday. This brother was astounded to find him hauling manure! Dad learned from this. As I was growing up the adults in our household fasted at breakfast time on Good Friday and spent some time during the morning in devotional activity.

So Dad enjoyed work. Yet how much of the work was pleasure and how much of it was necessity it is hard to know. The work was there and he did it, rising at 4:30 a.m. when his Westclox Big Ben went off and continuing until 7:00 or 8:00 p.m. or even later. There was time off, of course, for meals.

Before breakfast there was Bible reading, prayer, and a verse of song.

If he had not enjoyed work, perhaps he would have tried harder to avoid it with labor saving equipment. Yet he did innovate as time went on. His period of farming involved the mechanization of agriculture in the eastern United States. In plowing he went from the horse drawn walking plow to the three-point hookup. In haymaking he progressed from the pitchfork through the hayloader to the pickup baler. In grain harvest he began with the horse drawn binder and threshing machine and ended with the combine which does it both in the field. However, he grumbled once that with more advanced equipment you had to do more work to finance the equipment so the effort, he said, was much the same.

The work Dad preferred was dairy farming. I'm not aware that he had great affection for cows as individuals. Although they all had names, he could clobber them if they misbehaved. But he told me once that if he came home to the barn from the field tired, milking rested him. I myself never felt the same sort of affection for cattle care. So when on occasion he gave me a choice of continuing to operate the tractor in the field or going to the barn to feed the cows and to milk, I always chose to stay in the field. One reason for his preference for dairying was that in contrast to raising beef cattle, where the farmer might be paid once or twice a year, the milk check came twice a month. Even though it wasn't large, it was regular.

In addition to the dairy we kept laying hens for additional income. A problem with egg production in those days was the ease of entering the market. So the price of eggs fluctuated. When it went up the number of producers increased. Then the price dropped and a drop in production followed. Dad observed that the thing to do was stay in the business so one could profit from the highs as well as weather the lows.

Beginning in 1939, for eight or ten years we raised tomatoes for Campbell's Soup. But raising tomatoes was an annoyance in the yearly schedule of a dairy farm. In the spring setting out the plants conflicted with planting corn. In early summer cultivating tomatoes interfered with cultivating corn and harvesting hay and grain. In late summer there could be a lull on a dairy farm, but then the tomatoes had to be picked. And they were picked until frost, when you had to hurry and get the ground plowed in time to sow wheat. Tomatoes provided some stimulation to the cash flow, but I had a feeling Dad was glad to be done with them.

His work with tomatoes provided an occasion for Dad to put his foot in his mouth. At the Campbell's Soup plant in Camden, New Jersey, tomatoes were evaluated by government graders. They would take three baskets from a load and pay based on the quality they found in those three baskets. Some farmers were suspicious that graders favored the company, but this was the system and we had to work with it. Of most distress was an occasion when a whole truck load would be found unsatisfactory and rejected. This was more likely to happen at the end of the season, when quality could decline.

One year it happened to him. Uncle Milford came home with tomato seeds on his clothes and reported that a load of our tomatoes had been rejected. He had disposed of them at a dump part way home. This was about five tons of tomatoes and a significant loss. It stirred my father. He sent Campbell's an eloquent letter expressing his disappointment and possibly giving his opinion about their operation.

As a result they refused to pay him for other tomatoes already delivered unless he traveled fifty miles to Camden for "consultation." So he had to do it. As he reported to me, after the discussion he asked for the return of his letter. "Oh no," they said. "We will keep it in the file."

Life was difficult for farmers during the Depression, and the Roosevelt Administration wanted to help. I remember a man coming to the farm some time in the mid-1930s to offer governmental assistance. I don't recall what form the assistance was to take, but I presume it would have been a cash infusion. At any rate, Dad would have none of it. He was determined to make a living on his own without sucking the government's teat. He also refused a dairy subsidy during World War II. In later years when Social Security payments were mandated for farmers he paid under protest but declared, "I'll never collect."

One government program he did appreciate was the National Farm Loan Administration. Sometime during the 1930s the Hertzler family who had loaned money for the Pennsylvania relocation wanted the loan repaid. Dad was able to negotiate a National Farm loan. This had the advantage of a built-in repayment schedule so he was paying on the principal as well as covering the interest.

Then in 1941 a gas pipe line came through our area. The pipe line company had a smooth-talking front man to negotiate payment for rights of way and damages. The standard message was, "Take what we offer or we will go around you." Dad was not put off by such a ploy. With perhaps some informal counsel to arrive at a reasonable figure, he told the gas line company what he expected and they paid it. The payment was enough to liquidate the farm mortgage. In three more years my grandmother died and he had to settle with five other heirs. So back for another farm loan.

Because funds were generally short, Dad became adept at cutting corners, getting by with equipment that was less than top rank. In the early 1930s he and Uncle Milford bought an old Dodge two-door sedan for use as a farm truck. Since he felt he could not afford another vehicle for our family, the old Dodge served also as our family car. After a week with its right front and its back seats removed for hauling milk cans, sacks of feed, and sometimes a small calf, Dad would put the seats in again, and we would go to church in the Dodge on Sunday. For a small boy this was definitely low status transportation.

In 1937 Dad traded the Dodge for a 1931 Graham which had a luggage rack on the back. He had a wooden platform built to rest upon the rack so that the milk cans and feed sacks could be kept outside. The Graham sustained a major breakdown that summer. It evidently pumped oil, so Dad had new piston rings installed at a cost of $25. The new rings required a "break-in" period when the car was driven slowly.

Soon after this we left on a 325-mile trip to visit our grandparents who lived in eastern Virginia. Dad was not a high-speed driver and was no doubt being particularly careful during this break-in period.

But somewhere north of Richmond a 1935 Ford passed us. One of us children said, "There go Uncle Pauls. Let's catch 'em." Dad wanted to be a good sport, so he pushed down on the accelerator. With its new rings the Graham was not ready for this burst of speed and burned out a bearing.

Two years later Dad bought a 1935 Plymouth sedan and a 1929 Model A Ford roadster. The latter was to be adapted for use as the farm truck, so we finally had a car that was to be devoted solely to family transportation.

I never sensed that Dad brooded over or felt ashamed of being poor. He once quoted a saying to the effect that to be poor was no disgrace but *was* "unhandy." Yet he did sometimes become upset when horses balked, machinery broke down, or hired hands were less than fully functional. He regularly expressed his vexation by whistling—a doleful sound that made me uncomfortable and on occasion bemused the hired men. Also one time I overheard him reciting Scripture from Romans 5:3, evidently in an effort to calm himself: "Tribulation worketh patience and patience experience and experience hope."

About 1959 it occurred to me that Dad's years could be numbered. I began saving his letters. I find as I review them a repeated reference to being tired. He mentioned waiting to get up in the morning until he heard my brother Truman rattle the milk buckets. In one letter he wrote, "I find it something of a nuisance to be growing weaker as I grow older. This year I was unable to lift two bushels of wheat up and into the grain drill. Got along fair with barley." Then I recall that wheat weighs sixty pounds to the bushel and that he may not have weighed more than 125 pounds at this time.

Although he seemed to have difficulty devising a grand scheme for managing the farm, Dad could always find work for me. From filling the wood box I graduated to carrying milk from the stable to the milk house. After this came "stripping" the remaining milk from the cows after the milker was taken off, then running the machines and washing them. In all of these my highest priority was to get finished as fast as possible. Years later when Truman began to care for the dairy and wash the milkers, he took more time and got the bacteria count in the milk well below the standard. Truman is more deliberate in his work.

Most of the time as the oldest son I sought to do what was expected of me, trying if possible to get finished with the milking in time to get to the house by 6:45 p.m. to hear Lowell Thomas's newscast on Grandma Hertzler's radio. But one chore did frustrate me: cleaning manure from the cow stable with an old wooden wheel barrow. (Today I suppose the wheel barrow would be an antique, or at least a "collectible.") Because of his own energy Dad probably did not appreciate what drudgery this was for an early teenager. It caused me to contemplate running away from home, although I never got really serious about it. Just contemplated. Another source of discouragement was being sent alone into an eighteen-acre field to pick corn by hand. The year I left home, Dad hired a mechanical corn picker; I was a bit cynical.

At least until I was married, I never went home but Dad found work for me, which I found a little annoying. But then it occurred to me that it exhibited a kind of continuing acceptance. I could come home and move right into the system.

For my first twenty-one years Dad was the most important influence on my life, particularly after my mother died. Her death made him take his parental responsibility more seriously. I believe it was in 1937 when we were on a trip to visit my grandparents that I heard him tell someone his wife had died and he was taking his "babies" to visit her parents. I was eleven and did not appreciate being labeled a baby.

My first experience in Sunday school was at the Conestoga Mennonite Church west of Morgantown. But soon we began to attend an afternoon Sunday school at the Rock, a small meetinghouse near Elverson, which was being reopened after years of neglect. Some families took their children to church and Sunday school at Conestoga in the morning, then also to Rock in the afternoon. Dad evidently thought once a day was enough for us children, so we went only in the afternoon. Before many years the Rock moved toward becoming a separate congregation and held morning services.

Each year a revivalist came to our church for a week in June. This was an awkward time for farmers, but Dad always took church activity seriously. As a child I evaluated the speakers on the basis of the stories they told as illustrations in the sermons.

Then when I was about ten, Dad wondered if I had considered responding to the revivalist's invitation. (At Conestoga, they would organize an occasional membership class, but at Rock there was more emphasis on the evangelistic "invitation.") I responded, "Well, no. I hadn't thought about it, heh, heh." But later something hit me. So I raised my hand timidly one evening. The revivalist didn't notice, so I went forward after the meeting and identified myself. In due time I was instructed and baptized as a member of the congregation.

The age when young persons raised in Christian homes should be expected to declare themselves continues as a subject for discussion. One might suggest that at the age of ten mine was a response to adult pressure and that I should have had another five years of maturation before being confronted with the issue. At this point I would only say that the decision called for continued testing, but from it I never really looked back. I am glad to have been a member of an organization concerned to represent Jesus Christ.

At convenient times Dad warned me about issues I might be expected to face: cigarettes, sex, and booze. It occurred to me later that he never said anything against cigars, pipes, or chewing tobacco. Was this because he felt that the initial effect of tobacco in these forms was more violent than cigarettes and so considered them less likely to become habitual?

About booze he was so concerned that he would drink nothing out of a bottle. He told me once of an occasion when a neighbor wanted to treat him to a bottle of soft drink but he refused it. Why he was so definite about this I never learned for sure, although I did notice that he had a cousin with a drinking problem.

My membership in the congregation had an impact on my experience in school. After I was baptized Dad perceived that I should no longer salute the flag. At this time the state of Pennsylvania mandated an exercise at the beginning of the school day which included ten verses from the Bible, the Lord's Prayer (in the Anglican version), one verse of "America" and a salute to the American flag. Dad told me once that he had a teacher somewhere in his school experience who made the flag salute an important issue, and he had reacted against it. He discussed the question with a minister of our congregation, who was open-ended about it.

But Dad persisted. As an obedient son, I began to simply stand without saluting. As time went on, others in the one-room school joined me in this nonparticipation so that the teacher became frustrated. Instead of picking on me she chose a younger boy from another family. One morning she barked, "John, salute the flag."

John responded, "Ain't apposed to." Then the teacher complained that she had consulted teachers in another school where Mennonites attended and learned that they saluted the flag. She could not understand why we were so obstinate.

My high school principal, it turned out, was a Mennonite minister and he saluted the flag, so for me it became a moot issue and Dad no longer pursued it. As an adult I have vacillated on the subject, but my current general practice is to stand but not salute. Whether this is an important issue calls for discernment; it may be that the appropriate response will vary depending on the time and context.

Another place where the rubber of sectarian practice hit the secular road involved clothing. It was understood in our congregations that all male members should wear plain coats. Not all did, but we heard that Bishop John S. Mast would not baptize a man (or boy) without a plain coat. Some, it was noted, soon went back to a conventional coat, which was tolerated as long as they wore a bow tie, not a four-in-hand.

So when I became a member of the church, my coat was adapted. As it happened I made the highest average score in the eighth grade examinations for Robinson township. (At this time Robinson had one-room schools but we were brought together in the Birdsboro High School for these final exams.) The person with the highest score was expected to give a recitation of some sort at the township schools' eighth grade commencement.

At this point of venturing into the world I was sensitive about my peculiar coat so I wore a sweater to the rehearsal. (I was certainly no sharp dresser.) On the evening of the commencement, the eighth graders from our one-room school went early to the program with our teacher. The teacher's mother brought me a conventional suit coat, and I wore it that evening.

Dad was pretty upset and expressed his displeasure to me on the way home. "Well," I explained, "Mrs. Zerr brought this coat around." I don't recall that we ever discussed it again. However in one of Dad's last letters to me I noted a pensive reference to how others were changing their clothing style. "Most everyone receiving light and changing their looks.

Suppose a few old men will wear out their clothes. Maybe it's no use." I never found an occasion to mention that I too was adapting my style of coat.

In 1942 his hired man was drafted by the U.S. Army and Dad perceived that I should quit high school after two years and work on the farm. I was then sixteen and no official permission was required. I simply rode my bicycle away from high school at the end of my sophomore year and never went back.

Dad was very directive about this. He did not ask me whether I wanted to quit (I really would not have chosen it) but indicated that this was the way it was to be. However he did indicate that after the emergency I could expect to go to school again. So I could see a future in it.

Dad himself was a high school graduate in Tennessee and, I believe, president of his class. I think he knew some things about the effect of the high school peer group that he did not want me to learn. And he was clearly in need of help. No doubt there would have been other solutions if he had looked for them, but I don't have the impression that he looked. So I began a five-year stint as an adolescent farm hand while World War II played itself out.

Adolescence for me was a typical wasteland. An article I later published in *With* magazine was titled, "Seventeen Was the Worst Year." As I put it in the article, "It is hard to remember but I think seventeen was the worst year of my life. Or maybe it was eighteen or nineteen. As I say, it is hard to remember."[22]

Two issues related to life with Father are mentioned in the article. One was the transportation problem. The Rock and Conestoga congregations were twin congregations. Today we might say that Rock was a church "plant" of Conestoga. Being older, Conestoga had traditions to which Rock was expected to adapt.

As an Amish Mennonite congregation, Conestoga continued the Amish practice of bi-weekly young people's "singing."

Among the Old Order Amish the morning worship is held only every other week and the young people's singing follows in the evening of the same day.[23] At Conestoga Sunday school and worship were every Sunday and a Sunday evening program every other Sunday. This left the alternate Sunday evening open for the young people's singing.

At Rock a Sunday evening meeting was held on the same evening as the singing. Dad once protested this conflict to some church leaders but they responded, "The young people must have their singing."

The singing was a remarkable social and religious happening. For young people of the church community it was the place to be. Leadership was charismatic (that is, not elected). Someone negotiated a home for the next singing and if needed the word about the place was passed around informally. All songs were religious and anyone who wished—and was able— was free to lead a song. When it was deemed that the singing had gone on long enough—perhaps as long as two hours— someone would lead "Blest Be the Tie That Binds" and the formal meeting was over. After this there was time for chatting and then those who had dates took them home. I do not recall that the hostess was expected to serve food at these gatherings.

The conventional wisdom in our farming community was that a farmer would buy his son a car as soon as he had a driver's license. In response the son was expected to work for the father until he was twenty-one. But at least he had his own "wheels" to go to the singing. Dad was not one to follow conventions such as this. Instead he paid me modest wages.

I saved money and after a period of traveling to the singing in the farm truck ventured that perhaps I could buy a car. Dad reacted strongly. "I think you would be very foolish to buy a car," he said. He pointed out that a car began to depreciate as soon as you had it. Of course he was right, particularly during World War II when war production had taken precedence over auto production in the U.S. But at seventeen—or eighteen—

his reaction filled me with something less than joy. I had to continue to attend the singing in the farm truck.

Another issue that sticks in my mind after some years was the matter of suggestions. I had an occasional idea about how I perceived the farm practice could be improved. No doubt some of these ideas involved spending extra money. The memory I have is that Dad was open to none of them. At one point I thought of him in adolescent terms as "the most contrary man in Berks County."

I went along with his conservatism. What else could I do? But at points I took my stand. For example, although I worked with horses more or less under protest, I never harnessed one. Why should I learn this out of date chore? Today I recognize that horses enjoy certain ecological advantages over tractors, but we were not sensitive to that issue in those days. I found, of course, that at about the age of twenty-one these matters became of less concern to me. "It's his farm. Let him run it as he wishes." And soon after this my destiny led me in another direction.

At the same time Dad could be generous. As I noted above, he paid me wages from the time I began working full time. Also he granted me time off to pursue personal interests. In 1945 I attended the six-week special Bible term at Eastern Mennonite School and in 1946-1947 I went to Poland and then to Greece on cattleboats. This program was a part of a United Nations relief operation to help those countries rebuild their animal populations after the war. It also served as a way for farm boys to do some good along with seeing the world. These absences threw an extra burden on Dad, but he was open to them. However, before I went to Poland he warned me "Remember who you are!"

In the last year I worked for him Dad made me a partner in the farm operation and this meant a significant increase in wages. If I had chosen to stay with him I could have begun building an equity for a future in farming. I believe Dad considered the possibility that I might return to the farm after higher education. I was not completely closed to this, but the details never came together.

So it was my brother Truman who became the farming partner. His style was different from Dad's. He evidently represented Grandpa Shenk's precision and so was able to deal with technical problems that Dad and I would have needed to assign to others. But he was not the obedient first son. I heard him say that he felt oppressed by what he perceived as Dad's over direction in the decade they worked together. Yet Dad had respect for his ability as revealed in a letter to me. He wrote that "Truman can do most anything with someone to encourage him."

Dad was troubled by ulcers in the later years of his life. In 1955 Truman had to return early from his honeymoon because his father went to the hospital for emergency surgery. He never seemed really well after that. Nine years later he had surgery to remove his stomach because of cancer. He did not get out of the hospital alive.

In his last letter to me he reported that an X-ray had revealed an ulcer. "Dr. Mack said, 'I wish you to understand we think it serious. I have a bed for you Monday and operation Thursday.' I asked could I wait a few days for there are some jobs I would like to see out of the way. If I don't feel worse may wait a week. Would try and live with it were not for the threat of cancer. At seventy I suppose I am worth $1,000 plus and some months loafing. Of course possible my operation not successful but if it is likely be in hospital over Thanks Day. You can enjoy your visit without me. And I can still say, 'Cheerfully Grandpa.'"

I made two calls on him in the hospital during our visit, one of them on the way home. A few days later came the word that he was gone.

Several things about the funeral activities have stayed with me. Among these is my reaction to his body at the time of the "viewing." I have never been able to make up my mind regarding the importance of the body in mourning. But I noted several things at that time. For one he could have used a hair cut before he died and so his appearance was characteristic. Dad had straight, stiff hair and was wont to rub a hand through it for no apparent reason. (My youngest son has this same practice. Are such things passed on genetically?) So his long hair looked natural.

The other thing I noticed was a blood blister under one of the finger nails. This symbolized his life of hard work. As I remember, one of the jobs he wanted to do before he went to the hospital was to clean manure out of the heifer pens.

As for his funeral, my reaction to it was the exact opposite of what I remember from my mother's funeral some thirty years before. At thirty-nine I was glad for the presence of friends and relatives and was able to weep openly. One small advantage of facing death as an adult instead of a child.

After Dad's death I found it took me about six months of thinking about him to get my memories in order. During this period of remembering I wrote an editorial in which I said, "I have pondered his life and asked myself what manner of man he was. I find that the picture that comes back to me is filled with contrasts, perhaps even a few contradictions. As a book or a symphony has one theme but many variations, so Dad's person and experience combined a variety of characteristics."[24]

Since then I have read Paton Yoder's characterization of Dad's grandfather, John S. Stoltzfus and asked myself if he may have inherited his intensity from his grandfather. It seems almost as if there was a fire burning within him. George R. Brunk had "banked" it, but in times of pressure it would flame up. Such a time that I remember from my childhood was the visit of some Jehovah's Witnesses to our farm. Dad denounced them and verbally drove them off the place.

I witnessed a final flame-up a few days before he died. He did not care for the water in the hospital, so Truman agreed to bring him water from the well on our farm. On the day Truman and I went to visit him Truman forgot the water! I felt a little sorry for Truman. It was almost as if he was a small boy who had let the cows get out.

I do not wish to overplay this intensity. It was only one of the instruments in his personal symphony. What I admire about Dad is the easygoing way he handled money. Yes he should have been more efficient, but I doubt that anyone ever called him greedy.

Although he may have never gotten the farm mortgage fully paid off after 1944, he was solvent when he died. He left a small estate and his will included Mennonite Board of Missions as one of the family. One reason his legacy was small was that he was giving money away as he went along.

His attitude toward giving is symbolized for me by his reaction to an accident. He and a neighbor met head on at a blind corner half a mile from his home. As I recall, it was only a fender bender and both vehicles could be driven away. It was the sort of collision where each party might agree to cover the cost of his own repairs. But Dad took the initiative. "Well Dave," he said, "Get your bill ready."

I found it sort of comforting that the eleven-year-old Ford he was driving at the time of his final illness in 1964 had a probable street value of less than $100. At the conclusion of the editorial I wrote after his death I suggested that "To call him a 'success' one would need to revise the rules a bit. But his very carelessness about things that seem so important in our society may be a parable for those who can accept it."25

4

Ten O'Clock Scholar

I was late to school in 1932—six weeks late! It was no fault of my own. One of the childhood diseases was present in our family. I don't remember which it was—measles or mumps maybe—but in those days a household was quarantined for these diseases. A health officer posted a sign on the front door and children were expected to stay at home until the sign came down.

Eventually it was discovered that the quarantine did not help. By the time the child "broke out" others had been infected. So today when a child's little friend gets chicken pox, parents say "Uh-oh. In two weeks it will be our turn."

Actually I was a year and six weeks late to school. My mother perceived that it was better to keep me at home a year after I could have legally begun school. So I was seven when I began first grade. This meant that I was a little older than some of my peers as I worked my way up through the school system. And school was easy for me—at least in the grades.

I recall that in third grade—I believe it was—spelling was so easy I did not bother to study. Then one day I met a word I didn't know and blurted out that I hadn't studied. The teacher had observed this and was not sympathetic. So I had to do the best I could and came up with "kiten."

Kahler's School was a one-room building three-quarters of a mile from our home. All students walked to it except in emergencies such as rain. There were twelve double seats in two rows for a capacity of twenty-four students. We began in the front of the room as first graders and worked our way toward the back year by year.

Heating was by a pot bellied stove with anthracite coal for fuel. The teacher served as janitor and I recall on occasion she had the stove red hot. Also it was discovered that horse chestnuts put in the stove would explode and I believe boys once or twice tried this stunt, but not very often.

The school day extended from 8:30 a.m. to 3:30 p.m. with two 15-minute recesses and an hour-long break at noon. We carried lunches and in mild weather ate outside. We sometimes traded sandwiches—my strawberry jam for another's bologna. Since our family never bought meat, bologna seemed special to me.

There were no organized athletics. We organized the games ourselves. Someone had buried stones on the playground for a small baseball diamond where we played baseball with a sponge ball. Some boys hit the sponge so hard we added a handicap—hit it too far and it became an automatic "out." (I was not one of those boys.) Baseball was coed as was sledding. A quarter mile from the school was a pretty good hill for sledding. However, no one had a watch and it was sometimes hard to hear the school bell. The teacher got upset when we were late.

A popular game among the boys was "Hidin' an' Huntin'." This game depended on the woods and fields that surrounded the school. There were two teams and one team was given a few minutes to hide before the other one came to hunt them. All members of the hidden team must be found, run down and tagged to complete an inning. If not all of them had been tagged by the end of a free period, they were given time to hide at the beginning of the next period. I could not imagine how one could be happy in a school without fields and woods surrounding it. But as I moved on in education I discovered that it was possible to survive in other sorts of systems.

Three teachers monitored my first eight years of formal education. There was Miss Houk for the first three years. (Married partway through, she became Mrs. Witman.) Then there was Miss Binder for fourth grade and Miss Zerr for the rest of the way. Miss Houk, of course, taught me to read, using Mother Goose tales as our first reading material.

The school's library was limited. All the books were contained in one cupboard the size of a single kitchen cabinet. I probably read all of the books in it. At least I recall that Miss Binder was concerned about the limited selection and brought me books from her Sunday school library. I was a little surprised to find that one of them was *Tarzan and the Apes*. This did not strike me as the sort of book one would expect to find in a Sunday school library. But it was less harmful than a set of jingoistic war stories in the school library. In one of these fictional rewritings of history the Germans had invaded the U.S., captured New York and were advancing across Pennsylvania.

I remember confessing to Miss Zerr at the beginning of fifth grade that over the summer I had forgotten how to do long division. She assured me that we could soon deal with that problem and, of course, we did. In retrospect, my education in the 3Rs seems to have been adequate. We had little orientation in either music or art, but since I was not proficient in either one, I did not sense these omissions as a great lack.

In a one-room school, considerable responsibility rested on the teacher and it may be that students who needed extra help did not get it. I did observe that there was some supervision of the teacher. Mr. Moll came to visit the school occasionally and, perhaps once a year, Mr. Kemp, the county superintendent of schools, would appear. He was an acerbic man with a high pitched voice who seemed to enjoy tormenting the older students with puzzlers such as "What is the difference between a 'discoverer' and an 'explorer?'"

A school to which students walked was less subject to the vagaries of the weather than today's consolidated schools that depend on bus transportation. If the teacher could get to the school it was a school day. I do recall one marginal day in 1936 when my sister Katherine gave up and went home. I kept on through snow drifts up to my hips. The school was not really warm that day and Miss Binder wore her snow pants all day!

In addition to a basic education, the school system was concerned for our socialization, to have us become good U.S. citizens. This concern was apparent in the presence of two etchings that dominated the room. One was of Washington, the other of Lincoln. There were also the morning "exercises" which I have mentioned earlier. I suppose I was not entirely conscious of it then, but as I look back I recognize that my family and my church provided an alternate set of values and an assumption that the system symbolized by Washington and Lincoln should be kept at arm's length.

I had several Sunday school teachers who impressed me: Willis Glick and Elmer Stoltzfus. I think the value I found in them was the opportunity as a small boy to relate to someone other than my father. I later had a falling out with Willis over my going away to college. He predicted a time to come when people would not be able to buy or sell without the mark of the Beast and he considered it less than prudent to leave the farm. I don't recall having seen him since that time. However, I did see Elmer occasionally and had the opportunity to thank him for his teaching. He seemed bemused when I mentioned that all I could recall of his teaching was the remark that he thought it was all right for boys to take a "dip" in the creek on Sunday afternoon.

I remember finding Sunday school basically an enjoyable experience and recall on one occasion being impressed by a statement in a lesson book that the human body is beautiful. What better place to get a little sex education than in a Sunday school book? I hope the writer did not have to answer to some angry constituent for giving children too much too soon. The main negative element I remember from Sunday school was being called to the front at too advanced an age to sing children's ditties. I found this an onerous chore and for whatever reasons I dislike most ditties and choruses to this day. I find my best expressions of praise in the hymn book. Sunday school also emphasized reading the Bible. I began reading the Bible at age eight or nine and it has been a valuable resource throughout my life.

And so I moved on to high school. Robinson Township had no high school but the Caernarvon township line was only a quarter of a mile away, so Caernarvon High School at Morgantown was the place to go. A bus came by but it stopped a mile away, about half as far if I crossed the fields. Dad bought me a bicycle as payment for my work on the farm during the summer of 1940 with the understanding that I would ride it the four miles to school and thus could do more work at home before leaving. But in colder weather I rode the bus.

I do not recall my high school years as particularly notable. I do remember the names of three out of five teachers. Noah Good, a Mennonite minister, was principal and taught general science and German. Alvin Alderfer, a Church of the Brethren minister, taught social studies and biology. Dorothy Schott Groff taught English and algebra. I do not remember names of my Latin teachers, possibly because they changed between my freshman and sophomore years. My memory is that the teacher of freshman Latin was thorough, perhaps stiff, and our sophomore teacher let us off too easily. It was her first year of teaching Latin and our second year of studying it, but the combination did not add up to extensive learning.

High school was not hard for me, but it called for more focused attention than grade school. I took satisfaction from not having any home work except library books for required extracurricular reading. However it became apparent that some subjects took more effort than others. Algebra, for example. On one occasion the school board was visiting and Mrs. Groff asked for a volunteer to work a problem on the black board for the benefit of board members. It was a problem in what was colloquially dubbed "hit and miss" factoring. I volunteered but found that I almost couldn't do it. I finally collected my senses, got through the problem and retired to my seat with some embarrassment.

I became a celebrity for a day once during my sophomore year when the school held an information contest. Each class was represented by a girl and a boy. The seniors and the juniors all had to pass on the first question, but I was able to handle it. The answer was "Brazil" but I don't recall the question. This beginning was symbolic for the sophomores won the contest. A girl named Dorothy (I think) and I held out to the end and then she answered the final question and won the contest.

Roy Stoltzfus became famous in another way. A candy company with a product called "Mallo Cup" did a promotion by inserting letters in the packages. Anyone who submitted a complete set of the letters "Mallo Cup" would receive a case of twenty-four cups. Roy took the challenge. He ate a few extra cups, raided waste baskets and bought an additional letter or two to make up the total. He got his case of cups and I believe he reported that they all had the letter "M."

Caernarvon High School had an athletic program but I was involved only marginally. In part this was for lack of ability and otherwise because work awaited me at home after school. I never had time even to observe a full game.

Like Kahler's Elementary before it, Caernarvon had a good basic academic program. There were few frills, but after two years there I had ten credits of the sixteen required for a high school diploma in Pennsylvania. I had a pretty good foundation in English and social studies. I had studied biology and explored the mysteries of algebra. But when I rode away from the school in the spring of 1942 I turned my back on physics, chemistry and higher mathematics. I also passed up the opportunity to study a modern foreign language when I was young enough to lap it up easily. (Perhaps the last was no great loss. Some twenty years later I studied German on my own and learned enough to pass a university exam. What I needed next was the opportunity to live in Germany for a year and practice it. That chance never came.)

Except for the Eastern Mennonite School Bible term I mentioned earlier, formal education for me was to be postponed more than five years. Not that this was an intellectually dead period. I took several courses by correspondence: agriculture, economics and if I remember correctly, American history. In agriculture I learned that cold air is heavier than warm and runs down hill. So you can expect frost sooner at the bottom of a hill. Also one of my teachers inoculated me against the "etc" fault. In an assignment I had used this abbreviation freely. He circled every one and I have not been comfortable with etc. ever since. It is, if one stops to consider it, a rather useless collective.

There were things to learn from the farm work itself and, as I wrote in the last chapter, the opportunity to interact with my father in the trials that develop between a teenager and his parent. There were farm papers to read (*Farm Journal*, *Pennsylvania Farmer*, *Rural New Yorker*) and some books. Among these was *Mennonites in Europe* by John Horsch. Dad bought this at Weaver's Bookstore in Blue Ball, Pennsylvania (next to the harness shop which Weaver also operated). I have no memory that Dad read the book, but I did and it gave me a beginning sense of a Mennonite identity more extensive than what I had experienced. Two trips to Europe on cattleboats opened their own sorts of windows.

And so, over the hump of the forties, I was free to go to Eastern Mennonite College. It was not necessary to finish high school. My entrance to college was confirmed through a battery of tests given in the early days of the first semester. Perhaps they were the equivalent of today's SATs. At any rate, I was not out of place. Numbers of other students had their education delayed by the war. Some had no high school at all.

That I would some time go away to school had been assumed since the time of my birth. At that time some persons gave money and this was deposited in the Elverson National Bank as the beginning of an education fund. It wasn't much for a long time, but the idea was there and as I earned money during the five-year interlude, I added to the fund.

To go away to college did not fit with the unwritten rules of our Amish Mennonite community. I do not recall anything said against it, but only a few did it. Among those who had preceded me was Grant Stoltzfus, who was to become editor of *The Mennonite Community* magazine and later to teach church history at Eastern Mennonite College and to write *Mennonites of the Ohio and Eastern Conference* (Herald Press, 1969).

As for our family, the expectation of going away to college was evidently based on the fact that my parents had been "school people." I wrote in an earlier chapter of my mother's attendance at Eastern Mennonite School. My father too had been in school: he spent the 1916-1917 year at Goshen College. This is documented by three photos and by the freshman class list in the 1917 issue of the college yearbook, *The Maple Leaf*.

He appears in photos of the freshman class, the Aurora Literary Society and the Chemical Society. I got the impression that if he had continued in college, he would have majored in chemistry. But World War I sent him back to farming and that was where he stayed the rest of his life.

I was just short of twenty-two when I entered college in 1947. Late again. But I was to find that having gone back to school I would not get far from it for a long time. By the time I was forty I found that half my years had included time in school. And I received a sixth degree in my seventieth year. But this is to run ahead of the story.[26]

I entered college without my educational goals sharply defined. I was set to go to school but the questions of what to major in and what to do afterwards were not urgent. I believe Dad cherished the hope that I would return to the farm after school and I had no firm opinion about this.

Some persons I knew were enrolling in the five-year integrated Bible and theology curriculum. This seemed like a worthwhile program and so I signed up for it. I do not recall that we received any counseling from anyone about what to do. The program was there and we entered it. The requirements included one course in either mathematics or science. Considering my limited experience in math and my lack of physics or chemistry, I elected biology. Recently I was comforted by a remark of C. S. Lewis who confessed that "I could never have gone far in any science because on the path of every science the lion Mathematics lies in wait for you."[27]

College biology contained little math and although it was an intensive course, I did well enough that Daniel Suter invited me to become a laboratory assistant and to change my major to biology. I gave the invitation some thought but I was already a year and a half into the integrated Bible program and the thing to do seemed to be to keep on with it. The idea of biology interested me enough, however, that I have occasionally reflected on how my life would have been different had I gone into it. I think I would not have been unhappy doing so. And without majoring in it I have been able to maintain contact with things biological. Included in my interests are reading *Natural History* magazine, bird watching and planting a large garden.

A second intensive course I took that year was elementary New Testament Greek. The teacher was Dorothy Kemrer, the textbook was by J. Gresham Machen and the method was memorization of vocabulary and word forms. I understand that biblical languages are taught today more inductively. Whether this is less painful than the Machen method I do not know. I do recall that several students had particular trouble with the Greek language. Our style was every man for himself, but I have wondered as I reflected on this experience what would have happened had we tried a more community approach to the study. Could those who found it less difficult have tutored those who found it heavy going and so both received a satisfactory grade with reasonable effort?

Some fifteen years later at the University of Pittsburgh I was hit with my own version of these other students' dilemma: Educational Research 201, a course in statistics which I could not master on my own. If it was not a bear, it was a near relative. So I hired a tutor and with his help got through the course, but I remember it as one of my least pleasant educational experiences.

The entry into college in 1947 of numbers of persons whose education had been delayed put a strain on lodging. Students lived in several places off the EMC campus. One of these facilities was a former turkey house made available by Jacob Shenk, a friend of the college. My first year in college I was lodged in the turkey house. There were perhaps 20 of us and we had a sophomore, Henry Swartley, as student manager of this dormitory. Because it was a self-contained unit, the college rules were not enforced as stringently here as on campus, although Henry did wake most of us at 6:00 a.m. for morning prayers. I seem to remember that one room declined to participate.

Some persons prepared their own breakfasts in the dorm, but those of us who ate in the dining hall had to be there by 7:00 a.m. Dining was family style and there was no mercy for latecomers. However, the doorkeeper would hold the door open as long as anyone was in sight. So we would jog the quarter mile from the dorm to the dining hall, exhorting each other to "string out" so that those at the end of the line could be seen.

As noted above, the "integrated" curriculum included more than Bible study. It introduced us to areas of education commonly called "liberal." In addition to math or science we studied English composition like all the other students, plus English literature, history, and sociology. Also, as part of Introduction to Christianity, Stanley Shenk helped us learn to write research papers. This was a skill that I was to practice many times throughout my educational pilgrimage. Although a student's research paper may interest none but the student and the teacher, a basic principal of learning comes into play in the act of preparing such a paper.

Most of the teachers I had during five years at EMC were reasonably competent and contributed to my maturation and development of skills. But as I reflect on the end of the five-year program and what it eventually led to, I think particularly of two. John R. Mumaw taught sermon construction and sermon delivery. What I later learned about preaching through study and practice rested on a foundation laid in those two courses. And C. K. Lehman was a teacher and mentor who, like Miss Binder in fourth grade, got me books from his alma mater, Union Theological Seminary at Richmond, Virginia. Among these was Karl Barth's *Romerbrief*. Barth's writing was pretty heavy going. I should take a look at this book again and see whether I could make more sense out of it today.

By today's standards, the atmosphere of the EMC campus in the forties was regimented and solemn. This did not particularly bother me as I had come to college to study. The main dormitories were locked at night and any resident student who wished to leave the campus at anytime was expected to get permission. Lights were "out" at a specific hour and a manager patrolled the hall. Except for the sophomore year I was able to avoid this last regulation. Hours in the turkey house were less regulated and by my junior year upper classmen were allowed to go to bed when they considered it time to do so.

I was involved in one "stunt" during my early weeks at EMC. One social event as part of orientation was climbing Massanutten, a ridge to the east of the Shenandoah Valley. It was a vigorous hike, but no great challenge for young men off the farm, particularly when we were taken by truck to and from the mountain. During an early class period Stanley Shenk remarked that when he was a student they would hike from the college to the mountain and then climb it.

This stirred Myron Augsburger and he wanted to do them one better. On September 30 of that year, a moonlight night, he proposed a night hike to Massanutten and up the mountain and challenged someone else to go along. I took him up on it and Henry Swartley said if we were dumb enough to do it he would not stop us. So we took off jogging and arrived at the mountain in good time. We got to the top in the middle of the night and lay down to rest. But it was too cold to sleep, so we soon descended.

With several stops along the way for Myron to sleep, we arrived back at the dorm by 5:00 a.m. and at 6:00 Henry Swartley rang the bell for prayers! We did not have a particularly good day. Myron slept in Introduction to Music and in the afternoon I had a softball game in which I remember playing poorly. From a remark made later by a faculty member I gathered that we were the subject of discussion by the faculty, but that seemed to be the extent of it.

Except that it got into the college tradition. In 1966 when Myron was inaugurated president of the college, the student newspaper carried two articles related to the Massanutten hike. One recalled a number of his escapades including "the nocturnal dash to Laird's Knob [actually the wrong peak] and back for morning classes [that] established his renowned energy." The other used it as an example of his "athletic interests." It told how "one night about ten o'clock not too many years ago two young men left the dorm at EMC, jogged five miles across the valley to the base of Massanutten Peak, climbed the peak, and returned in time for breakfast the next morning."[28]

At about 3:00 a.m. on October 1, 1947, when Myron appeared to be walking in his sleep, I would not have predicted that he would some day become president of the college.

There was dating at EMC and, like other aspects of our lives, it was carefully monitored. I was in no hurry for dating. I had come to college to study. Also, although I had no problem with girls in general, I was awed by them in particular. But into my second year it seemed time to do something, so I invited Mary Yoder to the performance of Handel's Messiah at Bridgewater College. And she accepted! Although my social skills were certainly not well developed, I found a wife in college.

It is said that next to marrying a person from one's home community, college is one of the better places to find a spouse. Here you are likely to find a person with values similar to your own. As it turned out, she was a farm girl from northeast Ohio, and I a farm boy from southeast Pennsylvania. She was a preacher's daughter as my mother had been. We were both members of the Ohio and Eastern Mennonite Conference and after we became engaged someone pointed out that we were seventh cousins.

Mary had enrolled in the Junior College Bible program and so graduated three years before I did, followed by three years of correspondence between us. When we married she had no professional training, but, as I was to learn only gradually, a long list of artistic and practical skills. We have been able to make each other reasonably happy for more than 40 years, although I am embarrassed as I look back and recall some of the pressures my work imposed upon her.

After five years at EMC I had two bachelor's degrees, one in Bible and one in theology. I had no money, but no debts. The savings fund supplemented by summer earnings had carried me through. There were no automatic openings for degrees such as mine, although the Eastern Mennonite Mission Board contacted me and might well have assigned us. Also, Ira Kurtz, the bishop of my home district expressed interest in having me serve in that community, but they ordained by lot on the basis of congregational votes. "You have been away," he observed, "and it may be that no one will think to vote for you." So much for the power of the old time Mennonite bishop.

So I did farm work in Ohio until there came a call from Mennonite Publishing House, a call I will describe in a later chapter. At this point I will review the additional education which my work in publishing stimulated me to undertake. Less than two years after I was first employed at Mennonite Publishing House I went to school again. It was suggested that I do this to round out my biblical education by studying at Goshen College Biblical Seminary. So in a year and two summers I completed requirements for my third bachelor's degree, a Bachelor of Divinity, which was at that time the standard degree for ministerial training.

By now I had a wife and son, so attending school was not as simple as before when I packed up at the farm and headed off to college. During the first summer I left my wife and son to fend for themselves with some support from the extended families. In the fall I took them along and we moved into student housing. My wages continued in part (I believe it was half), Mary did babysitting to help meet expenses, and the tuition was modest indeed.

A memo I wrote on July 26, 1955, summarized total expenses for the second semester and summer school. It came to $593.75, less a scholarship of $125.00. Mennonite Publishing House covered half this cost so my bill for this education was $234.37! For this price you would scarcely get through the door of an educational institution today. Of course the half time salary I was receiving during this educational interlude was about $30.00 a week.

The two sessions of summer school which I attended in 1954 and 1955 were cooperative efforts between Goshen College Biblical Seminary and Mennonite Biblical Seminary which at that time had a campus in Chicago. These beginning cooperative efforts led eventually to the joint location of these two seminaries at Elkhart, Indiana, and ultimately merged. The 1954 summer session convened at Goshen. In 1955 we traveled to Chicago for one term, then back to Scottdale where I finished requirements for the degree by two "reading" courses with the grades based on book reports I submitted to Goshen. A month after we got home Mary gave birth to twins.

At Goshen, as at EMC, there were a number of helpful teachers but three stand out in my memory. H. S. Bender in church history, Howard Charles in New Testament studies, and John W. Miller in Old Testament.

For the next four-and-a-half years I was heavily occupied with family and housing activities. When our twins were born we lived in a four-room apartment on the third floor of the Mennonite Publishing House. About the only good thing to be said about the facilities was the price of the rent. I had built chicken coops on the farm so I set out to build a house. I found that it was a more complex operation. However with extensive help from H. Ralph Hernley and Stanley Yoder (at $1.50 an hour) and volunteer work from a number of others, we moved into our new house on January 1, 1957.

By 1960 it was back to school again, this time commuting to the University of Pittsburgh, mostly on a part-time basis. Soon after our fourth son was born and my weekly absences put a strain on the family. I sought to ameliorate the situation by bringing home children's books from the Carnegie library and generally taking classes between September and April, leaving the summer schedule more open. But in some years the school work spilled over into the summer. And most of the time I carried a full work load at Mennonite Publishing House.

No one told me I needed to enter this educational program. Although Mennonite Publishing House provided an educational subsidy, this school work was not strictly required for the work I was doing. Yet I sought to apply the learning where possible to my editorial efforts. The need was in me—a need to understand better and to sharpen my skills. It may be that I should have relaxed and built personally on the education I already had. But I chose the route of more education.

After six-and-a-half years I had finished the program and received the degree. Now I was a doctor, although as we joked at graduation, not the kind of doctor who "helps people." Yet I had conducted a survey of the comprehension of theological education among adults in a sample of Mennonite Sunday schools. I hoped it would help us in providing more usable Sunday school lesson materials. Whether it did would be hard to document. I believe it did make me more sensitive to the importance of clarity in the communication of the gospel. Probably this is about all that should be expected from an educational program. When one stops to consider it, what can we say is gained from years of education? As I reflect on this question a few things come to mind.

1. *Focused learning.* Going to school provides an opportunity to concentrate on a subject more than one is inclined to do when studying alone or simply observing the passing scene. In some cases what has been learned in life needs to be corrected. In others teachers can build on a foundation of what we already know. In graduate school the learning is more focused. The idea is to study one field intensively so the student becomes an expert of sorts in that field.

As they work their way up to this understanding, students absorb information and learn skills. The skills generally involve some form of surveying so that they can collect and concentrate data in a manner no one has done in quite this way before. They may even aspire to the status of the author of Psalm 119:9: "I have more understanding than all my teachers."

2. *Observing teachers.* Yet the guidance of teachers should not be despised. My final stint in higher education was undertaken after I had retired. Certainly at this point no one told me I needed to do it. But I felt that I had some unfinished

business and wanted to observe how teachers were doing it. I did take a little counsel before I began the program: I asked my pastor, I asked my wife, and I asked my son Ronald. All seemed positive and this gave me encouragement to do it.

3. *To be "at home."* My final program became an opportunity to fill in a few rifts in my knowledge of the Bible. I had majored in Bible in college and in religious education in graduate school. Yet there were large areas of the Bible which I had not studied intensively. I gave it a final push. The result was to make me feel more at home in a number of areas related to the Bible. Two for example.

One course I took was in biblical archaeology. Students were required to choose and study one specific "mound" in the Bible lands. I chose Tell el-Hesi, an obscure hill in southwestern Israel with evidence for human occupation from modern times to earlier than 4000 B. C. I worked on the geography and history of this mound. By the time I was finished I began to have a personal identification with it. If I should have an opportunity to visit Israel again I would like to see it. Not for itself particularly, but for what it symbolizes about the struggles and failures of mankind to find security in fortifications.

My final effort at Pittsburgh Theological Seminary was a study of the parable of the sower in the gospel of Mark. So what do I know now about the parable of the sower that I didn't know before? As with Tell el-Hesi, I have an at home feeling about this parable which I did not have before and I will continue to develop this relationship. It is *my* parable.

So in going to school one finds that subjects that were once strangers become friends. You may even be able to do business with them. It takes effort, it takes time, it takes money that will probably not then be available for high priced automobiles or stylish clothing. Certainly few can spend the time and money on formal education which I have done. If everybody did it the whole system would break down.

Yet as the world is flooded by information, formal efforts to understand and even to resist this flood will be called for. These can be done in any setting from Sunday school to the seminary. The urgency is highlighted by the words of Ephesians 4:12 and 14, where the leaders of the church are called upon "to equip the saints for the work of ministry, for building up the body of Christ" so that we should "no longer be children, tossed to and fro by every wind of doctrine."

Surely some sort of educational program will be required if the church is to carry out such a sweeping mandate.

5

The Mennonite Dream

The congregations in which I grew up were understood to be members of the Ohio Mennonite and Eastern Amish Mennonite Joint Conference. Amish, of course, was our tradition. Why Amish Mennonite? The addition of Mennonite identified us as among those Amish who in the nineteenth century began to build meetinghouses and make other adjustments to modernity. This separated them from those who came to be called "Old Order Amish."

The Conestoga Amish community near Morgantown, Pennsylvania, first built a meetinghouse in 1882. But already five years earlier they had expressed their intent by leaving a group that objected to fellowship with congregations west of the Alleghenies. From here had come progressive ideas, such as meetinghouses. According to J. Lemar and Lois Ann Mast, the division was not hostile but became final. "The two groups gradually drifted farther and farther apart until there was no spiritual interchange. However, both groups continued to help each other through tragedies and even today, when a barn fire strikes a member of the community, all work together."[29]

The Eastern Amish Mennonite Conference was made up of congregations from eastern Pennsylvania to western Ohio. John S. Mast, who became bishop at Conestoga in 1908, was a leader in the Eastern Amish Mennonite Conference.

As early as 1912 interest in merging the Ohio Mennonite and Eastern Amish Mennonite Conferences was expressed.

Bishop Mast was involved in these conversations, which led to a 1927 conference vote in favor of merger. But it was agreed that congregations were to be polled regarding the merger.

Grant M. Stoltzfus reports that twenty-eight congregations approved the merger, one voted against it and one took exception. Three congregations for which John S. Mast was bishop were not asked to vote. Mast "considered it best to defer action in his congregations but suggested that the committee proceed with the proposed merger."[30]

Bishop Mast's reasoning is quoted by Stoltzfus in a footnote based on a letter of October 5, 1928, more than a year after the merger had been formalized. Mast indicated his support for the merger, but he suggested the need for time before bringing the issue to a vote. He pointed out that he represented a district with some 700 members located between the Franconia Conference with 5,000 members and Lancaster Conference with 10,000. Members in his congregations were intermarried with Lancaster Mennonites. There were cooperative activities with this conference as well. The same relationships were involved with the Conservative Amish Mennonites.

"Because of location and church and family ties, Mast felt that 'by placing the matter of merging with the Ohio Mennonites before our people, some [may] say Lancaster Conference and others [may] say Conservative Amish.' By not submitting the matter for a vote at all Stoltzfus concludes, Mast here as at other times in his ministry, kept divisive questions from being debated and so retained greater unity."[31]

I find this of interest since, as I was growing up, I had a clear understanding that we belonged to the Ohio and Eastern Conference. How this was communicated I cannot recall. I am guessing that the question was never voted on but that the trust between Bishop Mast and our congregations made possible an assumed consensus without a formal vote.

A chapter on the bishop in the Mast history on the Conestoga congregation is titled "The Unforgettable Johnnie

S." Who but an Amish community would refer to their bishop with this sort of affectionate diminutive? Certainly not my father, who considered it important to refer to ministers with respect. If they were Mennonite, he called them "Brother." If not, he called them "Mr." He did admit to some difficulty keeping up this standard with a minister who was younger than he.

As I review the record, I find that Johnnie S. was a leader with more than parochial standing in the Mennonite Church. Grant Stoltzfus has more than a dozen references to him in his history of the Ohio and Eastern Conference. Most of these are routine, but one of them summarizes his work. It includes the dates of his life (1861-1951) and the dates of his ordination to the ministry (1894) and as a bishop (1908). Stoltzfus writes that "He played an important part in introducing the Sunday school, Bible conferences, sewing circles [!] and evangelistic meetings. As a leader in the more conservative part of the conference he was widely known and appreciated throughout the entire conference during the long years of his ministry."[32]

The Masts report that he had an early reputation for "his wisdom and ability in dealing with spiritual matters related to personal and congregational matters." Ohio, Maryland and Virginia are mentioned as areas where he served. "He was often asked to speak at special meetings, ordinations, as well as to settle difficult situations in various congregations."[33]

By the time I became aware of him, Bishop Mast's days for creative, forward-looking leadership seem to have been largely over. I remember him as an old man with a white beard when beards were not common. Also the Masts report that he injured a knee in the mid-thirties by falling on ice. As a result he used a cane which no doubt influenced my view of him.[34]

I am confident that he baptized me in 1936 as Mennonite bishops did in those days, although I have no specific memory of his ministry at that point. I do recall that in the mid-forties I approached him for approval of a literary society program.

He referred me to his associate bishop, Ira Kurtz, who had been ordained on March 7, 1944.[35]

Although I had little personal interaction with Bishop Mast, I was mightily impressed by his church discipline. It was specific and pointed and as a young church member I was filled with awe, if not with dread. The discipline was read twice a year at the members' council meeting which preceded the Lord's Supper. Each member was asked to give assent to it.

Certain details of this discipline stayed in my memory. However, to document these impressions, I searched for a copy of it. Through the help of Lois Ann Mast and C. J. Kurtz, a retired minister who had served with Bishop Mast, I received copies of two versions of the discipline. They support what I remembered: that it was divided into 1) recommendations or standards, and 2) tests of fellowship.

Among the recommendations were: 1) for brethren to wear a "regulation coat" without a necktie "and refrain from wearing anything that is only an outward adorning. Rom. 12:1, 2." 2) For sisters to wear a bonnet "of a square pattern," a covering, dark hose, dresses with plain goods and long sleeves. 3) Members were asked to avoid "mixed" bathing at beaches or swimming pools. 4) Also they were asked to "pay their honest debts," to" refrain from using or growing tobacco" and to "exercise extreme precaution" in the use of radios. (My grandmother had a radio. I think she exercised precaution in its use, but there may have been a couple of radio preachers who got money from her. She allowed me to listen to the Lowell Thomas newscast.)

Tests of fellowship included: 1) attending movies, 2) military service, 3) life insurance, secret orders, 4) strong drink and cigarettes, 5) "immodest apparel" or jewelry. Specifically for sisters these prohibitions included, transparent dresses, short skirts, "making a display of the hair. We ask our sisters to part their hair in the middle." For brethren other tests were going without a shirt or wearing a long necktie. It is not specified, but I understand that a "test of fellowship" meant that an offender was deprived of participation in the Lord's Supper.

There are other details, but these cover the main points. Reviewing this discipline after more than half a century gives me mixed feelings. For one thing, I find it interesting to note that "pay their honest debts" was a recommendation and smoking cigarettes a test of fellowship. If I could hear an interpretation I would understand better why it came out like this. No doubt it was hoped that members would follow both. This may have been the force of an item among the recommendations which stated that "members holding office in the church or Sunday school shall be in the order of the church." If "order" included the recommendations, defaulters on loans would not be asked to teach in the Sunday school.

I find it of interest that the ruling against cigarettes in this discipline anticipated by decades the 1964 U.S. Surgeon General's pronouncement against cigarette smoking. In this Bishop Mast was well ahead of his time. It would appear that he helped to save several generations of his people from illness and premature death related to cigarettes. As for why cigarettes were forbidden and other forms of tobacco tolerated, I suppose it was because cigarettes were modern. Would we say there was a kind of sanctified pragmatism in "grandfathering" older forms of tobacco?

In 1952 Mary and I transferred our church membership to Kingview Mennonite Church, near Scottdale, Pennsylvania. Mary's membership was transferred from Ohio and mine from eastern Pennsylvania. Kingview Mennonite was a member of the Southwestern Pennsylvania Mennonite Conference, which was soon to change it's name to Allegheny. Transferring our memberships was a routine matter. The bishop was satisfied with our manner of dressing and I had just been employed as an office editor at Mennonite Publishing House. Southwestern was a Mennonite—not Amish Mennonite—conference and had a conference based "Rules and Discipline." I do not recall that anything was made of these when we joined. I had to get into the conference archives to learn about them specifically.

I found that this set of "Rules and Discipline" was first accepted in 1882 and revised seven times, the last in 1954. The 1908 edition, a copy of which I found in the archives in Somerset, Pennsylvania, includes twenty-four items, beginning with *"Calling and Ordaining the Ministry"* and ending with *"Unity of Faith."* As indicated by Item I, the earlier items are procedural, but beginning with *"X. Head Covering"* and *"XI. Pride and Apparel"* the document speaks to a variety of behavioral issues. An example is XI. 2 *"Wearing of Beards—* Fashionable beards, such as mustaches, goatees, etc., are not tolerated in the brotherhood; brethren are required to keep the hair on the upper lip shaved off or closely clipped."

Item XIII includes a ban against holding "a license to sell spirituous liquors except for medicinal use." Item XIV deals with *"Worldly Offices."* This includes voting and on this issue "It is considered best that members not go to the polls to vote for worldly offices. We especially urge that the ministry and sisters refrain from voting."

Revisions of the document illustrate changing perspectives on issues, sometimes a softening or qualifying of a position. For example, on *"Using the Law,"* the 1908 version reads "no member is allowed to sue at law, or threaten the use of the law by posting notices, or otherwise." The 1954 version is more tentative. It says, "In our highly complex society the use of litigation is becoming increasingly more difficult to evaluate. . . . In the light of the way of love, we feel that the Christian should not become an aggressive party in a suit at law."

I have the impression that the 1954 revision of the "Rules and Discipline" was the last. This was probably because in 1963 the Mennonite Church accepted a new Confession of Faith and Allegheny Conference then elected to let this statement serve as a point of reference. This 1963 confession remains in print. However, in 1995 the Mennonite Church accepted *Confession of Faith in a Mennonite Perspective* which was prepared jointly with the General Conference Mennonite Church.[36] Following this development, Allegheny revised its constitution to read "The Conference is an organization within the Mennonite Church and accepts biblical faith as expressed in confessions of faith adopted by the Mennonite Church."[37]

Among the qualifications for congregational membership in Allegheny Conference is "The congregation confesses a faith common with our Mennonite Confession of Faith." What was once a specific statement has become part of a more general confession of faith. Is this a gain or a loss? I am not sure how to answer the question, but I find it interesting for this to have happened with few noticing.

However, James M. Lapp noticed it in retrospect. He wrote that "By the 1960s, the authority of conferences had waned in the Mennonite Church. Rules and discipline were quickly set aside in favor of more flexible approaches to discipleship." He notes also that "Not to be overlooked in this time of change was the growing individualism in North American society and the challenges to established structures and designated leadership in a church where the boundaries were eroding rapidly."[38]

It appears that we are part of a change in our culture observed by Lyle Schaller. He wrote that "The traditional emphasis in American culture on rules gradually has been eroded. The replacement has been a greater value placed on relationships.[39]

However, in the 1990s and beyond the question of homosexual practice emerged among us and brought about disciplinary action. Several district conferences of the Mennonite Church disciplined congregations which had granted membership to couples in same-sex covenanted relations.

The General Conference Mennonite Church has traditionally been more congregational and would leave the question of such an issue to the discretion of the local congrega-tion. As of this writing, efforts to integrate these two bodies have been put on hold as a result of this difference in church polity.

The 1995 Mennonite confession contains twenty-four ar-ticles on topics ranging from "God" to "the Reign of God." These include both doctrinal and behavioral statements. Article 17 is "Discipleship and the Christian Life." This article is specific about how Christians should be expected to live. "True faith in Christ means willingness to do the will of God, rather than willful pursuit of individual happiness," says the article. It goes on to mention, "simplicity" instead of "materi-alism" and "peace and justice" in contrast to "violence or mili-tary means." It supports "affirmation" instead of "oaths" and "chastity" instead of "the distortion of sexual relationships."[40]

One readily gathers that this confession is serious about behavior as well as doctrine. But the tone is less severe and pointed than particularly some earlier statements in the Rules and Discipline. Our Kingview congregation took note of the confession when it first appeared and preached our way through it. So we assume it as ours even though we may need to be reminded of it from time to time.

The most public statement of what we as a congregation consider important is given in a brochure entitled "Kingview Mennonite Church" which is available to visitors. Here we are identified as "persons who gather for support and nurture in our Christian experience" and "to praise and worship God for our salvation through Jesus Christ." Those who wish to be-come members are invited to join an "Exploring Membership" class. Here there is opportunity for us to speak specifically to issues that concern us.

I am confident that the Rules and Discipline represented earnest convictions. But some of the rules, it may be, were on the order of merely border maintenance. How important is border maintenance? There is no precise answer.

Border maintenance serves a number of functions. For one, it provides clarity on who is in and who is out—an identity function. For another, it serves to define appropriate and inappropriate behavior. A broader term than border maintenance is *nonconformity*, defined by C. J. Dyck as "the historic emphasis on Godly living and being in secular and often pagan society." Noting that Anabaptists took this perspective seriously, Dyck observes that in North America "geographical separation had largely disappeared. . . . Earlier boundaries were also no longer acceptable to the acculturated new generation. There was gradual or full conformity to social customs in regard to dress, wedding bands, recreation, automobiles, farming equipment and other externals."[41]

This sort of "acculturation" is apparent in our Kingview congregation. Although there are radical expressions among us and our position on following Jesus and living peacefully is clearly stated in our brochure, our general appearance is quite conventional.

I wore a "plain" coat until near middle age, then gradually laid it aside as others of my peers were doing. We had no major discussion of this. On reflection, I regret that we did not discuss this instead of skulking around like guilty children, wearing one sort of coat at one place and a different one at another.

I remember two experiences which suggested to me that clothing does not give a clear message. At one time I wore a light blue suit and on one occasion was wearing it on a public bus. I got the clear impression that a person I was speaking to perceived me as in the U.S. Navy.

"All right," I said to myself, "I will look the part." So I bought a dark suit. Then I had a conversation at a professional meeting and it came to me that my conversationalist viewed me as an Episcopalian clergyman. So much for the message of distinctive clothing.

It is possible to make too much of such ambiguities. There are numbers of Mennonites and Amish who eschew conventional clothing and devise their own costumes. There are also conservative Jews and others who have distinctive attire. But at this point in my pilgrimage I do not have great enthusiasm for it. I do believe however that it is possible to subvert the dominant paradigm in various small ways by simply refusing to follow the conventional wisdom in anything from automobiles to clothing, cosmetics, food, furniture and housing. Traveling in countries where people struggle for absolute necessities is useful to remind us that much of advertising is hot air. For myself, I make a mental note to avoid as much as possible anything advertised on television.

During an interlude in my work on this chapter I read two volumes in the "Mennonite Experience in America" series: *Mennonites in American Society, 1930-1970,* by Paul Toews; and *Vision, Doctrine, War,* by James Juhnke, which covers 1890 to 1930. I found it of interest to see how Toews who is Mennonite Brethren and Juhnke who is General Conference Mennonite would view our own Mennonite Church.

They seek to be fair and to respect our efforts to be faithful while pointing out places where personal ambition may have masqueraded as stated conviction. Perhaps because he is farther from them than some of us, Toews is able to respect the Old Order Amish and Old Order Mennonites. He does not consign them to a cultural backwater as some of us may be tempted to do, but suggests that they have a rationale for their rejection of modernity.

Yet as he observes, there is irony here. "In a culture nearly choking on consumption, the Old Orders maintain a frugal and self-sufficient lifestyle." On the other hand, "The ancestors of modern-day Amish were. . . . killed for their heretical ways. Today the Old Order Amish descendants of those martyrs are hunted down and photographed by long-range cameras roaming the back roads of Amish communities."[42]

Toews observes that Mennonites who have not chosen the severe cultural nonconformity of the Old Orders have replaced the older cultural symbols "with newer institutional, ideological and activist ones and with inter-Mennonite networks which nurtured the persistence of a distinctive Mennonite community."[43] So Toews points out that Mennonites have persisted with a separate identity in contradiction to a recent assumption by certain social scientists that distinctive communities would be swallowed by the forces of modernization.

"Into the 1970s both strategies worked. At least they helped Mennonites and Amish maintain an inner sense and self-identity of belonging to their own communities. And the Mennonite and Amish communities did not disappear into the larger American culture."[44]

I am identified with those who have chosen institutions and inter-Mennonite networking in place of Old Order nonconformity. Having grown up with aspects of the latter I sometimes perceive that we have gone too far too fast. Some among us have accepted aspects of modernity's cultural eccentricities almost without awareness. These complexify their lives in ways that can make them harder. The Old Orders have a point!

Yet when I reflect on the Old Order response to culture, I find one basic lack: an effective effort to make their faith "exportable." Conversion to the Old Order way of life is more the exception than the rule.

We are not so good at this ourselves, but during the last 150 years various groups of Mennonites have sought to be evangelistic. Some in doing so have given up on the Mennonite faith, particularly the offensive doctrine of nonresistance to the violent. But others have persisted so that today there is an international Mennonite fellowship of roughly one million members. This has only happened through the efforts of Mennonite missionaries who have attempted to make the Christian faith understandable. In this effort the Old Orders have not been much help.

My own view of the church is that it is by definition international. Yet parochial and national impulses keep getting in the way. Mennonite World Conference met in India in 1997 with some 4500 in attendance. Our Kingview congregation elected Kim Miller to represent us at the conference. Kim took along his wife Dianne and they brought back a report of the conference and of contacts with Mennonites in India which made our congregation a little more aware of the worldwide Mennonite membership.

In 1977 *Gospel Herald* published an article by David Augsburger entitled "The Mennonite Dream." It includes some of the more radical Mennonite ideas. Among them:

"A dream that it is thinkable to practice the way of reconciling love in human conflicts and war, nondefensively and nonresistantly.

"A dream that it is possible to confess Jesus as Lord above all nationalism, racism, or materialism."[45]

Such dreams are too high for us. We cannot expect to reach them consistently. Yet we perceive that the New Testament and our tradition expect them to be taken seriously and not to be sloughed off as impossible. Do we need a regular public reading of them to remind ourselves who we are and what we believe?

Not every Sunday or they might become over familiar and routine, but often enough to remember them. Of course we preach sermons regularly to stress what we believe. But sermons are eminently forgettable. We need something brief, focused, and memorable.

In reflecting on this chapter I ask myself whether I am obsessed with behavior at the expense of love—law more than grace. Perhaps I raise the issue because I resist the temptation to become an old man pining for the days gone by. In fact, I think I have indicated that I am relieved those days are gone. But by making so much of these behavioral questions, am I revealing the same mindset?

What interests one is the question of what sort of consensuses are needed in order for our churches to be clearly identified and as guides for our life together and instruction for our children. The Jews had the law and the prophets. Jesus summarized the commandments with two: love God and love your neighbor as yourself. But the Gospels include also quite a few sayings of his regarding behavior, some of which make us uncomfortable.

Paul in Romans and Galatians proclaimed that the law was finished now that Jesus Christ had come. But then he added his own list of suggestions on how the followers of Jesus should behave, illustrating how love should be demonstrated in life.

It boils down to the question of attitude. The late Donald G. Miller addressed a Reformation Day audience in our town some twenty years ago at a meeting, appropriately, in the Lutheran meetinghouse. He observed that Jesus, Paul and Luther all stressed that salvation is by faith. "But ask the average American on what basis he expects to be accepted by God and he will reply, 'I pay my taxes and I try to treat the neighbors right.'" Yet New Testament writers call for performance in both of those areas. The point is that such activities do not build up any sort of credit with God.

As I reflect on my experience in the Conestoga Mennonite community I recall that I seem to have been afraid of God until at least well into my twenties. Was this because of the church discipline or did the discipline only symbolize a whole atmosphere which caused me to tremble?

In occasional conversation with persons who were affected by this or similar discipline, I have observed resentment or remembered hurt. Certainly persons who have been to college and studied Freud, Jung, and Adler would find things to challenge. And did the church list of requirements overlook more important issues? When did we ever hear of someone disciplined for greed?

If in the past the church has been too specific and petty (I seem to remember that years ago young women were urged to wear nylon hose for baptism in our Kingview congregation) today we may be too mushy mouthed, assuming that people can figure out for themselves what the life of love requires. They do this, of course, with specific guidance from commercialism which urges them to indulge themselves.

Yet the dilemma is not new and it is of some comfort to hear an old comment from one who has been considered in the Christian tradition eminently wise. In Galatians 5:13, 14 Paul wrote "You were called to freedom . . . only do not use your freedom as an opportunity for self-indulgence, but through love become slaves to one another. For the whole law is summed up in a single commandment, 'You shall love your neighbor as yourself.'" I suppose we cannot get any more basic than this.

6

The Call

The call came from Paul Erb, editor of *Gospel Herald*. It came in late July 1952. It came during the day when I was away at work on a farm. When I returned in late evening, Mary said, "You are to return a call to Paul Erb."

I was surprised since I did not know him personally. We had met casually earlier in the year when he was an instructor during a six-week Special Bible Term at Eastern Mennonite College. I had traded barbs with him at a meal during his time there.

As conversation at the table I reported having met a strange character in Harrisonburg whose scheme was to ask people for "two pennies."

"Well," said Erb, "maybe he thought you looked as if you were worth only two cents." It was good for a laugh at my expense.

A few minutes later we were introducing ourselves. When his turn came Erb said, "I suppose you all know who I am."

"Yes," I replied with mock formality. "You are one of the Special Bible Term faculty!"

Our phone conversation that night was more friendly. "We have been checking around the church," he said, "and think we need you at Scottdale. Can you and your wife come to talk about it?"

This was a new development for us. Since my graduation in the spring and move to Ohio I had been working on a dairy farm for $125 a month. Before we married in early July, I received food and lodging at the farm. After our marriage I got instead gasoline to travel some twenty-five miles to and from the farm. Mary's father had taken a trip to Europe and Israel after our wedding and we lived for the time in his house.

I expected this job on a farm to be only temporary. But since when I graduated I had no significant debts—but also essentially no money—it was appropriate to work at what was available. Also, a small congregation in northeast Ohio wished to organize their own school and they looked to me to direct it. I am appalled to recall my naiveté in being open to such a possibility.

It was true that I had been to college, but the only "educational" course I had taken was Hygiene. As it happened, this was a requirement for both educational and theological students. Indeed the Th.B. degree I had received was not at that time readily marketable in the Mennonite church. But I had not gone to school with a career in mind. Rather I went for the love of learning.

So now I had a temporary job on a farm and had foolishly agreed to start a school. What should be done with Paul Erb's call? We went to Scottdale and were interviewed by what we were told was a "three-headed" committee: Paul Erb, Paul Lederach, and Millard Lind. It was pointed out that this committee directed three Mennonite Publishing House editorial functions: books, Christian education materials, and magazines. Each of the three was chair for one of these. The record doesn't quite document that memory, but almost. According to the 1953 *Mennonite Yearbook*, Paul Erb was chair of the Periodical and Book departments and Paul Lederach of the Christian Education department.[46] And in the 1952 *Yearbook,* Millard Lind is listed as chair of an Editorial Council.[47] So this is the evidence for the three-headed committee.

What they needed at Scottdale was an office editor for *The Mennonite Community*, a monthly publication at that time being edited by yet another committee. They needed someone to prepare materials for the monthly deadlines and work with printers during the printing process.

How they had perceived that I could help them was not made clear to me. I had no training in journalism. However, I had written a few things for publication at the college and had published one article in the *Gospel Herald*. It was "What Basis Nonconformity?" which appeared on October 10, 1950.[48] But what probably got their attention was my work as editor of *The Shenandoah*, the Eastern Mennonite College yearbook. It had been printed at Scottdale and I had mail contact with H. Ralph Hernley, chair of the committee which now edited *The Mennonite Community*.

How I became editor of the college yearbook represented one of those strange forkings in the road which affect a personal destiny. In spring 1951 I was nominated as president of the Young Peoples' Christian Association, a student organization at EMC that engaged in a wide range of mission and service activities. The other nominee was my brother-in-law, Willis Hallman. He was elected. He had previously been appointed editor of the yearbook, but college policy declared that a student was not permitted more than one major extracurricular assignment. So he was no longer eligible to serve as editor and I was appointed. I have the distinct impression this assignment started me on the road toward editorial work.

Now several important things happened within about a month. For one, a second farm job opened. It was located two or three miles from home instead of twenty-five and paid $1.25 an hour instead of $125 a month. As a rationale to my employer for resigning, I used the need for time to work on plans for the school I had been asked to develop. (Working from maybe 7:00 a.m. until 9:00 p.m. certainly allowed no time for any creative planning.)

The next important happening was a decision by the congregation not to begin a school at that time. They decided adequate funds were not available. This opened the way to accept the editorial assignment at Mennonite Publishing House without going back on a tacit agreement to work for the congregation. So we moved to Scottdale during the first week of September 1952.

I took a cut in pay to accept this assignment. My new rate was $1.05 an hour instead of $1.25 an hour as it had been on the farm. This rate was calculated on a maintenance basis as 85 cents an hour for me and an additional 20 cents because I was married. The policy also included four cents an hour for each child in a family. I was told this arrangement had begun about the time the publisher, A. J. Metzler's twins were born in the 1930s. It was to end sometime after our own twins appeared in the mid-1950s. In between three other sets of twins were born to MPH families. I have not heard of any twins born to MPH workers since that time!

Although wages were modest, so were living expenses. We had our choice of two apartments on the third floor of the publishing house building. We chose the four-room instead of the five-room since it was cheaper and seemed all we needed at that time. The rent was $22 per month in the winter and $20 in the summer, utilities included. After our twins arrived, we could well have used the larger apartment. Further, this was substandard housing. Well heated in winter, it became stifling hot in the summer. At one point we considered renting a larger apartment close to the Kingview Church. But we did not see how we could handle a rent of $50 a month.

Mary and I were Depression children. I had just come out of school, and she had worked as a domestic for modest wages. So we were used to skimping. I seem to remember that for a time our grocery bills ran $5.00 a week, and that I accumulated my bi-weekly checks and cashed two at a time. This doubling up ended a few years later when we had children.

When it had begun in 1947 *The Mennonite Community* was an innovation in Mennonite publishing: it used pictures extensively and for the first two years its publisher was the Mennonite Community Association instead of the Mennonite Publishing House. As H. Ralph Hernley remembered in the mid-1990s, MPH at that time did not publish pictures. (They are not completely missing if you examine the publications of that time, but photos were not emphasized in the manner *The Mennonite Community* was to do at the beginning.)

For the first year or two *The Mennonite Community* indeed emphasized pictures and had Paul W. Hertzler on the staff as "photographer and artist." But this position evidently became too expensive. By 1949 Mennonite Publishing House assumed responsibility as publisher. By the time I arrived plans had been made to merge the magazine with *Christian Monitor*, an older MPH publication. It was hoped this would gain enough circulation to become economically viable. By 1952 *The Mennonite Community* still used pictures but on a more pragmatic basis. In some instances we were reduced to amateur photos to keep down the costs.

The printing technology used at MPH in the early 1950s had changed little in more than half a century. Typesetting was done by linotype. According to *World Book*, the first successful commercial use of this system was in 1886.[49] This machine cast individual letters in a line of metal which had been heated from a metal bar by a gas furnace attached to the machine. These lines of type were subsequently locked into "forms" and assembled on the printing press where the actual type was pressed on paper.

Preparing photographs for printing required making metal engravings. Photos were sent from Scottdale to Johnstown for this, an operation that added to the time required to complete the printing process.

By the mid-1950s these methods began to change, first in printing, then in composition of the type. First was the arrival of an offset printing press that printed at least twice as fast by printing on every revolution of the cylinder instead of reciprocating as the older presses did. The images for printing had been engraved on an aluminum sheet and then on the press were transferred (or offset) to a rubber blanket and then to the paper. The actual type was no longer needed on the press.

But at first composition by linotype continued. After making corrections, the compositors prepared one copy of the material on high quality paper which was photographed and the negative used to make the aluminum plates. The type was then melted.

A more economical process was on the way, but when it arrived the only ones pleased were the budget cutters. Whereas the printing composed by hot metal had sharp, crisp edges, the first electronically composed type had fuzzy edges. Corrections might be a different density from the original type making the corrected lines sometimes appear as bold faced type. After several generations of composing machines the quality improved enough that linotype composition was long forgotten.

Mennonite Publishing House was in an expansion phase at the time I arrived. Soon after I came publishing agent A. J. Metzler reported that for the first time gross sales had reached $1 million. (By comparison its 1996-1997 income was $15.5 million with a margin of $35,000.[50]) A new organizational structure was emerging. There would be an editorial division, a sales division as well as a finance division along with the production division which had already been separately organized. Later a personnel division would also appear.[51]

Soon after I arrived, a planning group began to meet in preparation for the new magazine slated to replace *The Mennonite Community* and *The Christian Monitor*. It would be called *Christian Living* with the subtitle "A Magazine for Home and Community."

A staff of part-time editors supported the enterprise: Millard Lind, editor; Alta Mae Erb, home life editor; John A. Hostetler, community life editor. As assistant editor I performed a role similar to what I had done for *The Mennonite Community*: prepared material for publication and "steered" it through the printing process.

Month by month each editor submitted a group of articles. After I had prepared the assemblage for submission to the printers, Millard Lind examined the material. Most of the time he found it satisfactory, although I remember one occasion when he pulled rank on me. A cover photo I had chosen did not please him; he ordered me to replace it.

Each of the three "content" editors represented a specialty which informed their work with the magazine. In addition to editing, Millard Lind supported the magazine's theological or "personal living" emphasis. A seminary graduate, his other role at MPH was as writer of Sunday school materials for adults. Alta Mae Erb had a background in elementary education and was the author of a well-received book, *The Christian Nurture of Children*, first published in 1944. John A. Hostetler had a Ph.D. in sociology. His dissertation on "The Sociology of Mennonite Evangelism" had prepared him to think about social issues affecting Mennonites in the 1950s. For the rest of his time, John A. was book editor at Herald Press.

Each of these three received salary from *Christian Living* at the rate of 20 or 25 percent. As assistant editor, my salary was calculated at the rate of 7/11 or 63.63 percent. As I recall, this novel fraction had come from the publishing agent, A. J. Metzler. For the rest of the time I was employed as assistant pastor of Kingview Mennonite Church. The total editorial time charged to *Christian Living* came to something like 1.33 persons. My impression was that the administrative hope for the publication was to have it "break even" financially, but it seldom ever did. Also I recall that Millard Lind expressed hope that the magazine could reach a circulation of 15,000, but I believe it never quite attained this.

In addition to the paid staff the masthead listed three consulting editors: John L. Horst, Guy F. Hershberger, H. Ralph

Hernley. These men represented the concerns of the two merged magazines. John L. Horst had been the editor of the *Christian Monitor* for twenty-four years. It was not much more than a courtesy to include him. He was in the process of retiring from Mennonite Publishing House and soon moved to Harrisonburg, Virginia, where he lost direct contact with *Christian Living*.

Hershberger and Hernley represented the Mennonite Community Association, the organization that had been the original publisher of *The Mennonite Community*. With the community passing from the scene, they wanted to see the concerns which had brought the organization and the magazine into existence have continued emphasis. As described in the first issue, January 1947, it was to be a "paper which will emphasize and maintain the cultural, financial, and domestic life and culture which has been a part of our Mennonite life." This was the vision of S. F. Coffman, pastor of the Vineland, Ontario Mennonite Church.[52]

Hershberger, a professor of history and sociology at Goshen College, had a similar vision. As described by Paul Erb in that same first issue, "he too, got the idea of a magazine which should help Mennonite folks to see what a good thing we have in our religion-centered community life!" *Christian Living* was expected to carry on this vision, particularly in articles submitted by John A. Hostetler.

Another activity used by the MCA to air its concerns was a series of conferences on "Christian Community Relations." One way we found to mesh with the organization was to attend and report on these conferences. A report I wrote on the 1954 conference at Harrisonburg, Virginia, appears in the July 1954 issue of our magazine.

The theme of the conference was "Christian Community for What?" and Guy F. Hershberger developed the theme in his keynote address. Using Paul's letter to the Philippians as a text, Hershberger declared that "the church is a colony of heaven." Reporting on the speech, I summarized Hershberger's concern as follows: "He noted that Mennonite communities have certain commendable qualities such as fellowship, lack of sophistication and lack of specialization. But these qualities can be used for mere economic and social purposes which are not worthy goals. The only worthy use of Christian community resources is the spreading of the gospel."

After being a party to an extensive list of speeches, reports, and tours of Mennonite businesses in the areas, I concluded, "In the mind of this reporter, one of the most important things gleaned from the conference is the increased realization that Mennonites are rich and that apparently not all are sure what to do with their riches."

I suggested that "it is questionable whether Mennonites have a right to live in $30,000 to $60,000 houses and drive $3,000 to $5,000 automobiles. . . . Christian community for what? Personal comfort or the kingdom of God?"[53] After more than forty years it is of interest to consider how much one should inflate the figures for houses and cars to make the same point.

At the same time I wonder how many read the report and whether anyone considered it important. Did anyone consciously buy a cheaper house or car as a result of this conference or of my report? I have no way of knowing. An anomaly of editorial work was its relative impersonality. Like Henry Wadsworth Longellow's arrow, you sent a message into the air. In my experience, unless the communication was found offensive, I was not likely to get a response. Just the same, I kept on editing and writing. I did it because I saw the task as a call from the Lord and from the church through Paul Erb.

Indeed on one occasion I was representing the case of Mennonite Publishing House in the congregation where I had grown up. In my best public relations manner, I emphasized that MPH was a service agency. "We are there to serve you," I said.

Harvey Beiler, a lay leader in the congregation responded. "No," he said, "you are serving God." A straightforward reply, but a comforting thought, especially at times when the issues became delicate.

After a little less than two years of editorial work, I was encouraged to take a leave of absence and attend Goshen College Biblical Seminary. When I returned from this leave in 1955, the pastoral work which I had done on a part-time basis had been assigned to another and I would go back to full-time editorial work. In addition to magazine journalism for *Christian Living* I would begin to edit Christian education curriculum material.

The first sign of this in the record is my name as editor of Herald Uniform Sunday School Series in the 1957 issue of *Mennonite Yearbook*.[54] And in 1958 my name as editor appears on the mastheads of quarterly Bible lesson books for five different age groups. This would change in 1959 when the Herald Graded Series appeared for children and my work was restricted to materials for youths and adults. But for more than fifteen years editing curriculum materials would occupy a significant part of my work.

Editing curriculum material involved a different set of editor-writer relationships. If we were to use analogies, we might think of the magazine editor as a cross between a program planner and master of ceremonies. Magazine editors were prominently identified as directors of the operation. The work of perhaps a dozen different writers might be featured in a single issue of the publication.

A curriculum editor could be viewed as a midwife attending the development of a theological statement. As a rule, one person wrote all the material in a given issue of the publication. The writer's name was featured prominently. My name as editor appeared at the bottom of the title page following the names of the executive editor and the chair of the Christian education department.

By the late 1950s Millard Lind had withdrawn from curriculum writing to pursue biblical studies and later to become a seminary professor. So we began to engage pastors and Bible teachers as writers of the lessons. This was a change in overall strategy. For a number of years the writer of the Uniform Bible Lessons for adults had been theologian in residence at Mennonite Publishing House. He was a part of the MPH family, and available for interaction with Mennonite Publication Board. Now the writers would be out in the church or in another institution. Editing was assigned to a young untested editor. Trouble was on the way.

Among the writers we engaged was Clayton Beyler, a Bible teacher at Hesston College who had recently received a doctor's degree in New Testament from Southern Baptist Seminary. Clayton wrote a six-month series on the "Life of Jesus" which was first used in the churches the first Sunday in October 1958. With the lesson for December 14 we hit a snag.

The lesson title was "Jesus Shares His Ministry" and this Sunday had been designated as "Bible Sunday." The lesson text was Mark 6:6b-13 in which Jesus is found sending the twelve disciples on a mission. In a comment on Mark 6:8, Clayton wrote, "The instructions given to the twelve differ in details in the Synoptics and in a few points are even contradictory. These differences can best be explained as adaptations by the various evangelists to meet their peculiar situations."[55]

"Contradictory" was not a happy choice of word. It threw up flags so that some could not perceive the point Clayton wanted to make. Anyone who would have taken the trouble to compare the accounts would see that what Clayton wrote was true. In Matthew 10:10 Jesus tells the disciples to take neither sandals nor staff; Luke 9:3 forbids a staff; Mark 6:8-9 commands both staff and sandals. Sunday school people had not been used to examining the Scripture this carefully. John L. Horst came to my office and said, "Clayton Beyler is too young a man to say the Bible contradicts itself."

There were other problems of a similar nature, but this is the one which remains clearly in my mind. To make the issue more intense, Clayton had written a six-month series, not just three as writers usually did. At the turn of the year three more months remained in which to make us at Scottdale nervous. In a letter of February 16, 1959, to Paul Erb, J. Ward Shenk wrote, "Some of us were amazed to learn of the weak or almost nonexistent provision for doctrinal and practical safeguards around our literature. Yet you have the tenacity to question our judgment in exercising some choice in this area and this in the face of materials being foisted on the church from the pen of Clayton Beyler, to mention one example."

In my own naiveté, I was ready to talk with any objectors about the problem and would have welcomed an opportunity to get Clayton Beyler together with concerned persons and seek a common mind. Indeed, I was a little hurt to find that Mennonite Publication Board discussed and acted on the problem with neither Clayton nor me present. But maybe this was better since an issue so intractable might cause some to want to crucify the offenders if present.

As a result of this controversy we did not use Clayton as a lesson writer for several years. When we began to assign him again, we first used him as a writer of Old Testament lessons. I believe that by the time of his death in 1973 he had gained wide respect as a biblical expositor. Perhaps also his most ardent detractors had found other material.

The problem, of course, did not go away. How to interpret the results of biblical scholarship for people to whom they are new and threatening remains a delicate endeavor. One general principle is that this can be done more effectively in a classroom setting. If a class could have been led to compare the words of Jesus as reported in the three Gospels and pondered their significance, they could have been better helped to appreciate the issue and at the same time retain respect for the Scripture.

Even the covers could make trouble. I think it was Paul Lederach who had begun the use of religious art on covers of the curriculum pieces, and I continued this practice. Often it was of a classical nature, even sometimes medieval. But on occasion I discovered a piece by a contemporary artist.

An example was "Peter," by Sam Patrick, which I used on the cover of Herald Adult Bible Studies for October, November, December 1959. As characterized by Patrick, Peter was a stern balding man with a full beard. I perceived it as a representation with character. Martha E. Zook of Belleville, Pennsylvania, had another perspective. She wrote on October 28 of her "deep disappointment in the cover picture of the adult quarterly. Poor Peter. ..."[A little girl who attends our Sunday school] was so scared of that ugly picture that the mother had to keep it hidden. It haunted the child so badly that the mother finally tore the cover off."

It was some comfort to receive a letter from Mrs. Jesse Egli of Gilmore City, Iowa, who wrote that "'Peter' by Sam Patrick was a most pleasant surprise. It was entirely compatible with my own mental picture of Peter."

In the spring of 1991, six months after my retirement at Mennonite Publishing House, I returned part time as an assistant editor of Uniform Bible lesson materials for adults. After more than thirty years I was back in a role similar to what I had begun in the late 1950s. Once again I gave thought to the question of the lesson formula: what should be written to enhance biblical interpretation in adult Sunday school classes? How can the material be organized to get the attention for the biblical message?

Word came from the Board of Congregational Ministries at Elkhart, Indiana, that we should follow the "shared praxis" approach of Thomas Groome. Once I understood this, I built it into the instructions to writers of the Adult Teacher column in *Builder* magazine. This approach calls for beginning a Sunday school class with an opportunity for class members to share their own personal stories before going into the biblical text, so the text may speak to their personal concerns more than be thrown out on its own as an academic exercise.[56]

When adequately developed, this provided for a dynamic adult lesson period with discussion of everyday adult issues. However, when visiting adult Sunday school classes, I have sometimes observed teachers who seemed to prefer a static lesson plan, which is readily available in a nondenominational Sunday school magazine.

No storm of protest followed our efforts to use the shared praxis approach. But we did encounter a small hurricane over an offhand comment in a lesson on Genesis 1 in *Adult Bible Study Guide*. Like Clayton Beyler's 1958 observation regarding the accounts of Jesus sending out his 70 disciples, this observation in 1993 surprised and infuriated some people.

Gary F. Daught, a Mennonite pastor in Manitoba who had attended Union Theological Seminary in Richmond, Virginia, made the following comment regarding the creation account in Genesis 1:1-15. He wrote that "There is general agreement among students of the Old Testament that this account was composed while the Jews were exiled in Babylon from 597/587 to 539 B.C. Significant insight into the intentions of the author(s) can be gained by understanding the impact the exile had on the Jewish community."[57]

I thought this was a reasonable statement and as an editor did not challenge it. On reflection, I should have considered whether there might have been a way to make the observation in a less inflammatory manner. Unlike Clayton Beyler's observation, which could have been documented readily, "There is general agreement among students of the Old Testament" was difficult to deal with. Of course in both cases the objectors evidently did not wish to deal with the evidence.

What we ran into in this case was a longstanding tradition that Moses wrote Genesis. Indeed a copy of the King James Bible which I have in my study titles it "The First Book of

Moses called Genesis." Possible echoes of this tradition appear in the New Testament, as for example in Luke 24:27, "Then beginning with Moses and all the prophets, he interpreted to them the things about himself in all the Scriptures." Yet this text does not specifically say that Moses composed the books. Nor is Genesis itself credited to Moses. Indeed, Nehemiah seems to be the only Old Testament book of which the authorship is clearly identified.

Yet Moses and Genesis have been tied together like hand and glove. A file in the editorial office on this problem is close to two inches thick. Included are copies of letters from me, from David Hiebert, at that time editor of *Adult Bible Study Guide*, from Nelson Waybill, divisional coordinator. Included also is a statement that Gary Daught, David Hiebert, and I released expressing "regret" for "the confusion this has caused in our Sunday schools" and inviting "all who have a perspective on [this subject] to write to us."

This apology and implied openness to dialogue was too tame for MPH management. They took the essence of our statement, captioned it "We're sorry" and bought advertising space in the *Gospel Herald* to get the message out. The final sentence in the statement was from us: "In issues of controversy more than one position should be acknowledged, and we failed to do so."[58] The reason we did not, of course, was that we did not perceive the level of feeling the statement would stir up.

Among the more sensible comments in the file is a copy of several pages from the "Introduction to the Pentateuch" in the *Jerome Biblical Commentary*. This author states that "The modern world has a rigid concept of the inviolability of an author and hence a repugnance to successive and extensive redactions of material over a long period of time, especially in the case of the inspired word. This concept was not shared by the peoples of the ancient near East, who practiced community in thought and in the written word."

As for Moses and the Pentateuch, "Without Moses, or someone similar to him, these facts would remain without adequate explanation. Moses therefore, is at the heart of the Pentateuch and can, in accord with the common acceptance of the ancient period, correctly be called its author."[59]

Not so long after this eruption I felt that the time was coming for me to end my part-time work as an editor. I proposed this to Levi Miller, the new director of the Congregational Literature Division. By fall 1994 they found they could function without me.

But in 1995 I was able to write an article on the Bible for a *Gospel Herald* series on "Confession of Faith in a Mennonite Perspective." In the article I contrasted the viewpoint of Genesis 1 with the Babylonian creation myth which held that creation came about through violence. In the Babylonian story, the gods were fighting and the earth was born in violence of the gods. I wrote that, "The writer of Genesis was most likely aware of this Babylonian myth and flatly rejected it. The faith of Genesis 1 declares that God was outside the creation process and that creation was good."[60] The Babylonian creation myth no doubt predated Moses. But it seems to me that the Jews would have most likely have encountered it during the Babylonian exile.

However, I did not put it out bluntly as did Gary Daught. I am not aware that the editor of *Gospel Herald* got any hot letters in response to my article. I do value the Bible and I agree that we need to try to take it on its own terms instead of imposing our own terms on it. It is an activity calling for our most dedicated efforts. Ultimately, it is what the call was about.

7

When Is an Editor?

The year 1960 was a particularly significant year for our family. In January I began to attend classes in religious education at the University of Pittsburgh. This program would take six-and-a-half years, ending in summer 1966.

In February I was appointed editor of *Christian Living* magazine, succeeding Millard Lind, who resigned to teach at Goshen College Biblical Seminary. He had already virtually withdrawn from work on the magazine and after his resignation executive editor Ellrose Zook said to me, "Well Dan, just keep on."

During that spring and summer, Mervin Swartzentruber and I added a garage and breezeway to our house. This relieved some inside and outside problems that had been with us since the house went up in 1956.

The fourth significant event that year was my ordination to the ministry in July. Although I had taken theological training and had served for a time as an assistant pastor, I had not been ordained. Was it desirable or necessary for an editor of church literature to be an ordained minister? I had no clear leading on the question, but I took the position that I would neither seek the office nor refuse it.

Mennonite Publication Board asked for my ordination and it was carried out by publishing agent A. J. Metzler in his role as Allegheny Mennonite Conference bishop. An ordination gift I received from Ellrose Zook was a copy of *The*

Preacher's Calling to be Servant by D. T. Miles. In front Ellrose wrote, "In appreciation of your fine editorial service and with sincere wishes for a continued successful ministry in Christ." I valued this vote of confidence from my executive editor.

Not everyone understood my status as a minister-editor. Some years later I was present in a meeting where we introduced ourselves to each other. I identified myself as a "minister of literature." This moniker surprised the group; they laughed. I had not intended it as a joke.

About two weeks after my ordination our fourth son, Daniel Mark was born. Finally in August, we bought a used car, a seven-year-old two-door Chevrolet 210. It was a low mileage car, just short of 30,000 miles, and was to become our family transportation for four years and 50,000 miles. We turned it in then for lack of space—six of us could no longer fit comfortably into it. Today almost anyone would be scandalized by how we traveled. No seat belts or child seats, the youngest standing on the front seat between his parents. It was several vehicles later before we had a complete set of seat belts. We are grateful we were able to avoid becoming statistics in someone's accident report.

As I moved into the 1960s I found myself with multiple responsibilities, including work, family, and the part-time graduate education I largely pursued between September and April, leaving the summer more open for the family. But at times special activities pushed into summer. One year it was a Christian education seminar at the University of Pittsburgh. Another year it was a thirteen-day group dynamics workshop at Green Lake, Wisconsin. Yet another year I studied German to take a qualifying exam.

I think it was in spring 1963 that I was invited to address Mennonite Publication Board on behalf of editors. I chose the title, "When Is an Editor?" Maybe the title was a little too "cutesy" at first glance, but as I developed it, I believe board members could see I had a serious intent.

I have not succeeded in efforts to find a copy of the address, but the outline is clear in my mind along with some of the details. The three points in my address completed the question raised by the title: 1) When is an editor preparing?; 2) working?; 3) successful? I used the occasion to emphasize certain ambiguities in an editorial assignment.

In response to the first question, I observed that only a minority among the editors at Scottdale at that time had been to journalism school. Most of us were not trained to be editors. Several had been teachers, and this was probably the most common professional background among us. I maintained that the question of when a person was preparing to become an editor remained open. I do recall now that executive editor Ellrose Zook had graduated from Syracuse University with a degree in religious journalism. But this had come after a lengthy career in other publishing related activities, beginning as a printing press operator in the middle 1920s.[61]

I asserted also that similar ambiguities circled around the definition of the editor's work. This, I think was related to the question of how much an editor should be expected to produce. Since all the editors in my generation had had some academic training, we probably looked to the academic field for models. The academic person, we understood, was expected to spend some time ruminating as it were, gestating some creative thought or project. When would such activity be editing? Or could it shade over into loafing?

I expect institutions with a heavy quota of academic types have had to labor over this issue. How many hours should a professor be expected to teach? At Mennonite Publishing House we found ourselves outnumbered in a production oriented institution where the number of "press impressions" at one time was routinely calculated. It may have been because of this that I felt called to emphasize the importance of creative brooding. Yet I need to acknowledge that in my own experience the amount of editorial material one could process fluctuated depending on the length of one's personal agenda. If one wished to take an extended trip it was possible to do more in less time to prepare for it.

My third question was perhaps a bold, even fool-hardy one. How to measure an editor's success? Yet the fact that the publication board invited me to address them only a few years after the Clayton Beyler controversy suggested they did not hold this controversy against me.

What did I offer as a definition of editorial success? I believe I mentioned that old editorial bug-a-boo, circulation. One obvious measure of an editor's success is the willingness of people to pay for the publication. A magazine editor's success depends on the ability to assemble a collection of material that will interest a specific audience and sell at a price they are willing to pay. This success is based on editorial intelligence and initiative combined with available resources.

To produce a fine magazine within MPH financial constraints to serve the limited Mennonite Church audience was in some respects a daunting assignment. To conserve resources most of us handled more than one publication. An article I wrote for the *Gospel Herald*, September 20, 1966, identified me as "editor of adult publications at Mennonite Publishing House. His responsibilities include *Builder*, adult lesson quarterlies, leadership training texts, and *Christian Living*."

One publication I declined to edit: *Mennonite Yearbook and Directory*. When Ellrose Zook proposed it to me, I jumped out of my chair in distress. He got the message and did not press the issue further. I am confident I could have worked with this publication had I determined to do so. But somehow the heavily statistical nature of the publication appalled me. Not that I did not consider it an important publication. Indeed, today I use it, or its successor, *Mennonite Directory*, every week. But I did not see myself producing it.

As an editor, I sometimes had the opportunity to work with certain writers over a period of years. Some produced series of articles. Whether readers today would have the patience for such a series might be in question. But from February through July 1956 we published in *Christian Living* a hard-hitting series on "Christian Race Relations" by John David Zehr, pastor of the Calvary congregation, an interracial church in Los Angeles.

The series began with an article entitled "All of One." It stated that "The differences that separate mankind into races are superficial and minor compared to the unity of all men before their creator."[62] The second article, "The Brotherhood of Sinners" declared that "Civilized people are as depraved as the head hunters of New Guinea."[63] The final article of the seven was "The Sin of Race Prejudice." Its last paragraph asserted, "Race prejudice is sinful. It grows out of pride and self-righteousness. Racism thrives on misunderstandings, half-truths, and deliberate falsehoods. . . . Race prejudice is of the devil."[64]

Readers seem to have taken the series in stride. The only complaint found in the record was in response to the illustration I used for the second article. It was a posed stock photo which purported to show a thief entering through a window. Jacob D. Mellinger of Lancaster, Pennsylvania, wrote, "I was shocked when I opened my March number of *Christian Living* to meet a man with a gun in his hand, and to think that this magazine represents a nonresistant people.

"I do earnestly hope that this magazine does not stoop to give us pictures like this in future issues. How can this help but fire the innocent mind of a child for things military?"[65]

What sort of illustration might I have used to highlight such an article? A Currier and Ives etching perhaps? Something classical and thus less realistic? Cain killing Abel? Editorial work was always subject to review by readers.

Zehr later moved to northern Indiana and eventually became pastor of the Yellow Creek Mennonite Church, west of Goshen. From here he wrote a quarter of adult Bible lessons for me. The title of the quarter was "Old Testament

Biographies" and the first lesson was called "Joseph: Achieving Character."

I evidently felt that Zehr's description of Joseph as a youth could use some strengthening, so I added a phrase. As published, a comment on Genesis 37:3,4 stated: "In this passage one sees the normal family joys of a father in his son and the son in his father. But we also find that the passage describing Joseph's youth suggests that in some respects he was a teenage brat. However, these same Scriptures also show his solid moral character."[66]

A reader took exception to the expression "teenage brat," so I responded and sought to interpret what I thought John David meant to convey by the phrase. I sent John David a copy of my response and he replied that this was my term, not his!

In 1966, a number of us attended a writers' conference at the American Baptist Assembly, Green Lake, Wisconsin. We invited curriculum writers and scheduled special sessions for them. John David was among those invited, but he was killed in an auto accident on July 2 near Racine, Wisconsin. He was forty-three.[67]

A writer's career with a happier development has been that of Katie Funk Wiebe. In a communication read at the 1997 Mennonite Church General Assembly, Orlando, Florida, Katie wrote "I owe a great deal to the Mennonite Publishing House. My first connection was through Daniel Hertzler of *Christian Living*. I was just beginning to freelance. No word from him for a long time. Then I received a letter from him with a check for $5.00. But he returned most of my article. The check was for one or two paragraphs 'cut out' literally of the article. I still have the mutilated article somewhere in my files. But I was overjoyed. I had made my first sale!"

I could wish in retrospect that we had responded to Katie more promptly and more professionally. I cannot remember the details of this transaction, but I can imagine that I shared the article with Helen Alderfer, who was home life editor of the magazine. I would guess that we agreed this was not a very good article from a writer we did not know, but that it had a good insight which we could use as a short piece in the magazine. So we cut out the "insight," sent token payment, and returned the rest of the article.

It was a rocky start for Katie, but she did not give up. She would eventually become a regular writer for our magazine and has had six books published by Herald Press. As of 1997 five of them were still in print. Perhaps this is one of the more important indications of success by an editor: being able to mentor and develop writers who themselves make a major contribution to our readership.

The 1960s are remembered as a definitive period in U.S. history. This was the decade of youthful protest ("Don't trust anyone over thirty"), of opposition to the Vietnam War, of civil rights struggles, of the assassinations of Martin Luther King Jr. and of Robert Kennedy. I was not closely involved with any of these movements, although I do recall thinking that I agreed considerably with the youthful point of view. I was against war—all war—although my reasoning was not the same as some of theirs. Instead of "Hell no, we won't go," I would have said, "In the name of Christ, count me out." I had my own heavy agenda as described above: editorial work, graduate school, family life, and church activities. Some Mennonites did participate in civil rights activity. The closest I got was to be a sympathetic observer.

This has been typical of my work as an editor. I have been more in the background than the foreground. I would be more likely to report a demonstration than to participate in it. I have been an organization man, a committee member, a moderator of meetings.

A fourth question I might have raised in my presentation to the publication board would have been "When is an editor faithful?" Is it enough to help produce a publication for people to read? Is something more expected? I have found myself responding to requests for my services more often than going out and offering them.

Maybe this is the influence of my Amish Mennonite background: that one should wait for an invitation rather than push oneself forward. These requests have been regular: from my local church to the district conference and, occasionally, from the church at large. My identity has been formed in part by being needed.

My first assignment for Allegheny Mennonite Conference was to serve as assistant secretary and keep the minutes for the annual session in the summer of 1953. A recent assignment has been as chair of the leadership commission that holds credentials of ministers in the conference and organizes enrichment activities for them. As I reflect on the relation between editorial work and work in the church, I feel my editorial work has needed to be anchored in the church for which the published material has been intended. It has been hard enough to be authentic as a Christian without separating oneself from the people we publish for.

Editorial work was not as glamorous as some may have viewed it. Once or twice during my career I met people who seemed to want to touch an editor. If they only knew it, much of the work was simply writing letters, making phone calls, and pushing papers around. On the other hand, I once showed my office to a friend who was a farmer. I got the impression that for him to work in there would have been next to going to jail.

The reality was somewhere between these two perspectives. Editorial work was an opportunity to organize a set of materials on a regular basis, materials that made a statement about issues which we considered important. Sometimes there was direct feedback. More often I operated with only the knowledge that someone must be reading if the publications kept being renewed.

Like preachers and other performing artists, we as editors were always interested in feedback. From time to time we conducted a reader interest survey in an effort to document our hunches about what people found more and less interesting. We also published letters from readers when we could get them.

When I worked with *Christian Living*,it did not draw enough reader response to have letters in every issue. But occasionally we published something which hit some readers "crosswise"; then we got letters. Among the more colorful responses was a letter from one John R. Renno of Stillwater, Pennsylvania. He reported that in a conversation "I predicted (perhaps foolishly) that if you keep on going the way you have, in twenty-five years you will be advertising liquor, or at least cigars, in your papers."

What specifically concerned Renno was a photo of Rosalind Rinker published in February 1962 in connection with an interview by community life editor Victor Stoltzfus related to her book *Prayer, Conversing with God*. Renno wrote, "Rosalind's hair was just as short as a man's hair; indeed if she had not had feminine features it would be hard to tell what sex she was.

Renno was not completely fair. On the opposite page was a photo of a group of Mennonite college students at prayer with the women properly veiled. But evidently he perceived that we were giving Mennonite women permission to cut their hair. Whether our magazine had this kind of influence would have taken more sophisticated research than I could have designed.

A more extensive controversy surfaced in 1965 following an article "Was Christ Respectable?" by Martha Wagner published in April. According to her testimony in the *Gospel Herald*, March 2, 1965, Martha was "A Mennonite by choice and by the Grace of God." I thought her little article on Jesus made a point worth considering. A significant block of readers did not agree. "It was a fine piece of work for the devil," wrote M. L. Beyer of Kinzers, Pennsylvania. "It is the most ridiculous reading I have ever done," said Jeff Gingerich of Kalona, Iowa. Mrs. Evan Hartz of Hephzihah, Georgia, considered it "blasphemous and anti-Christ in the extreme."

These and other objections appeared in the July 1965 issue. I gave Martha an opportunity to respond. She tried to clarify her point: "If it means God-pleasing, then Christ was, of course, respectable. If it means man-pleasing, world-conforming, then He was not, nor should we be."

Some readers who saw these negative reactions to the article responded with support for it. A number of these appeared in September 1965 including from Myron F. Zerger of Dearborn, Michigan, who wrote, "In many of our Christian churches today Christ would be shunned if not excommunicated."

On occasion the feedback came years later. Not so long ago a woman of the next generation remarked that she and her husband came to their position on the use of alcoholic beverages on the basis of my writing. Since I wrote against them, I assume they decided that way. Otherwise she probably would not have told me.

In 1964 we celebrated the tenth anniversary of the founding of *Christian Living* magazine. After ten years, *Christian Living* was still operating with its original model: editor, assistant editor, and two department editors. But all the principals had changed. I was now editor, Loren Lind assistant editor, Helen Alderfer home life editor, and Victor Stoltzfus community life editor. Helen was a homemaker living in Scottdale and Victor a pastor in eastern Ohio. While on the *Christian Living* staff he began graduate work in sociology at Kent State University and eventually went into full-time academic work. From 1984-1996 he was president of Goshen College. Helen would continue as editor until her retirement in 1984 and in 1997 was still writing a monthly book review column. Loren

Lind later went to Columbia University School of Journalism and became a newspaper journalist.

We had a picture taken of the editors with their families. This seemed appropriate for a family oriented magazine. Looking at the picture after more than thirty years gives me mixed feelings. Significant changes have come to both the magazine and the families. Both have had to deal with the realities of life—some of them less than pleasant. Of the eleven earnest children's faces looking out from the picture, most have grown up to become responsible citizens in our culture. But one has died and others have been borne down with life's ambiguities. As families, we have not been spared the traumas of modern life.

We editors all made brave statements in that tenth anniversary issue about our task. We acknowledged the pressures of life yet maintained that there is a place for faithful living. Helen Alderfer observed that like a redbud tree broken by the wind, "The Christian family has been in a storm, too. But it is not about to be destroyed, for it has strengths to draw on."[68]

Victor Stoltzfus hoped to "avoid the temptation to religious faddism. When there is weakness in the life of a Christian group, there are usually shortsighted persons who propose a part of the Christian message such as church discipline, Christian experience, revivalism, small groups, Christian education, stewardship, service, holiness, and the tongues and healing movement as the one truth or method that unlocks all other truth. If it were only that simple!

"It is our purpose to be sensitive to all of these parts of the truth and most of all to be a part of Him who is the truth as we write and edit."[69]

As the oldest child in my family, I suppose I embodied the stereotype of trying to keep everyone happy. I don't remember serving in this role as a child, but in my work as an editor, I didn't publish simply to stir things up. It just sometimes happened.

If the subject was the interpretation of Christ this was delicate enough. If it was a report on present reality, this could be even more so. There is correspondence in the file from the mid-1960s involving concerns of editor, writer, subject, interested party. Should a subject be permitted to correct an article about her?

I allowed this privilege to Esther Eby Glass and the author Jane Lind, wrote, "If you had given me a chance, I would not have consented to printing the article as it appears now, because that is not how things were told to me." The writer's hurt is evident. She accused me of favoritism. "We have a scale of rating people. Depending on who the article had been written about, they would never had seen a copy, and depending on who it would have been, it wouldn't have mattered." I had fallen into an editorial trap from which there seemed no exit.

About the same time Jane's husband Loren Lind, who had studied at Columbia University School of Journalism, wrote a series of three articles on Mennonites in New York City. It was naïve of me to think that such a series could be done without incident. After the first article appeared, I received a distressed note from John H. Kraybill, who called attention to some factual errors and wrote, "I specifically requested that [the author] let me with some local person read the articles before publication to check them for their accuracy." He also was concerned that articles should be checked "not only for accuracy, but also to avoid any unnecessary offense in Lancaster County."

We got the second article through, but I concluded that the third could not be published, though I paid the author for it. I wrote to him that "to publish it would bring grave distress to some of our best friends in the Lancaster Conference. The Lord knows we have enough enemies there that we can hardly afford to lose all our friends."

He responded that he had seen the first two articles as basically publicity pieces, but in the third he was "touching the sensitive issues." (What these were I do not recall after thirty years.) He went on to express the opinion that "stirring things up is the whole function of Christian journalism. . . . It is ironic beyond comprehension that Christian journals fail on this point. They ought to excel, with all that is preached of honesty, truth and freedom. But somehow or other it seems that the church thinks of itself so much as the embodiment of these virtues that it sees no need to practice them."

When is an editor. . . .

Circulation of *Christian Living* was 14,327 in 1964 and it lost a modest $952, according to the publisher's annual report. It was to reach a circulation peak in 1965 with 14,695. After several years of decline, it gained 258 copies from 1967 to 1968 to 13,501. It would never be that high again.

In 1973 after twenty years with *Christian Living*, thirteen as editor, I was transferred to another assignment. *Christian Living* has had five different editors in twenty-five years, but it keeps reinventing itself and as I write is still being published. There is yet plenty to say on this subject and I am glad this magazine is seeking to say it.

8

To Look at and to Touch

Ben Cutrell became publishing agent at Mennonite Publishing House in 1960. He was only the third person to be called to this assignment. He followed Aaron Loucks, who began in 1908, and A. J. Metzler, who succeeded Loucks in 1935.

Throughout the 1960s Ben continued the organizational pattern which he had inherited and then began a new one with the year 1970. The former organization called for six divisions, three operating divisions and three service divisions. The operating divisions included editorial, production, and sales (later marketing). The service groups were curriculum development and service; accounting, finance and buildings; and personnel.

Ben's reconceptualization called for organizing along product lines. There would be book, congregational literature, and periodical divisions. Each of these was made responsible to market its own products. Production, finance and personnel divisions continued. A management information division was added.

Ben invited me to become manager of the Periodical Division. It was a task I had not trained for. My education had been in Bible on the one hand and in religious education on the other. Indeed none of the three new division managers had been specifically trained for management. So Ben sent Paul Lederach, Maynard Shetler, and me to Chicago for a seminar in business management. I hope it did some good. About the only detail I recall is that we were free to drink all the Pepsi-Cola we wanted and I have not cared for Pepsi-Cola since.

The Periodical Division as Ben set it up was to last until 1984. At that time four of the six periodicals were transferred to Congregational Literature Division. *Christian Living* and *Gospel Herald* continued as before until 1988. At this time the new publisher, J. Robert Ramer, terminated this division and assigned these last two publications also to Congregational Literature. As a separate division of Mennonite Publishing House, the Periodical Division lasted a relatively short time.

Ben's management style, as I would find, operated like the spokes of a wheel. Each of us was responsible individually for the management of our own division and we reported to Ben one by one. We did meet in a house council once a month where we processed institutional issues such as wages. But we seldom meddled in each other's work.

I generally had the feeling when I met with Ben that he was on my side. I observed however, that any time I began to criticize the printers his support became less firm. Then I recalled that he had managed a printing plant in Colorado before he came to Mennonite Publishing House.

After seventeen years at Mennonite Publishing House, I was ready for a new challenge although I would not have said that I had lost interest in what I was doing. My editorial work was divided between Christian education study materials on the one hand and editing *Christian Living* magazine on the other. After six and a half years of graduate study in religious education I would be leaving work directly related to this field. However, my dissertation had been a study of theological communication so not all was lost.[70]

Managing the new division was not considered a full-time assignment. I continued to edit *Christian Living* magazine. As I recall, the proportion was something like two-thirds time for *Christian Living* and one-third time for management. As manager, I saw myself as first among equals rather than as a top down administrator.

In the archives I found one sheet entitled "Opening Remarks" which was apparently my introductory speech to the division. The first point is titled "The Grand Design" and the notes say "There is none. It's up to us kids."

Point three of my notes states that "I assume about as much brain power per capita in this division as any. . . . I don't have any slick answers and business is new to me. I invite you to search with me. Some propositions to guide our department: We are not in business to make money, but we need enough money to stay in business." There the notes end. The rest of the document is lost, but this perhaps gives the flavor of my approach to management.

The personnel manager prepared a job description for "Periodical Director." When I saw the wide-sweeping nature of the presumed expectations, I concluded this was a document which should be suppressed. The "Primary Function" was stated as "Executes efficient general management in the planning, creation, and distribution of periodicals to meet House and Board objectives." That was certainly comprehensive but a little general. It had some wiggle room.

Then follows "Duties." The second paragraph in this category sets the tone: "Sets philosophy and priority of periodicals to be published. Determines educational, theological, and physical specifications of materials. Ascertains salability of product and sets circulation requirements. Provides for editing, writing and production of products. Selects appropriate methods of distribution, sale, and promotion of materials to meet circulation requirements." The rest of the document goes on in much the same fashion. I suppose I did this in a general way, but I was glad to see that it was never held up to me and used for a point by point evaluation.

The division as it came to me included seven publications. Two were adult: *Gospel Herald* and *Christian Living. Purpose* might have been considered youth-adult, *With* was for youth, *Words of Cheer* and *Story Friends* were for children. (*Builder* magazine, a publication for congregational leaders, was included at first because I was the editor but was soon transferred.)

Most of the time the editorial responsibilities called for each editor to do the work as an individual assignment. What should a manager be expected to do? Two responsibilities which fell on me were staff recruitment and preparing the annual budgets for the division.

Recruitment tasks faced me at the beginning. First, Paul Schrock resigned as editor of *Words of Cheer,* although he continued for awhile as editor of *Purpose,* his other half-time assignment. *Words of Cheer* was a weekly children's publication going back to 1876. (Like *Purpose* and *Story Friends,* it was largely distributed in Sunday schools.) At the same time there was a move among Mennonite Church agencies to call for enhanced news reporting by the *Gospel Herald,* which meant recruitment of a half-time news editor.

A corollary stirring called for the merger of *Words of Cheer* with a General Conference Mennonite (sister denomination of the Mennonite Church but at the time a separate one) publication called *Junior Messenger.* I understood that I was to find an editor for the combined publication. Frank Ward, executive secretary of the General Conference Commission on Education later told me I should have taken broader consultation in seeking this editor. His displeasure was evident. Without the benefit of that perspective, I went right to work on the problem.

Since 1958 Helen Alderfer had served as home life editor of *Christian Living.* The Alderfers moved to Scottdale that year when Helen's husband Edwin became pastor of the North Scottdale and Kingview Mennonite churches. For the year 1969-1970 Edwin and Helen took leave from their assignments. He studied at a school of pastoral care at a Baptist hospital in Winston-Salem, North Carolina, and Helen taught school in that area to provide family support. During Edwin's absence the two congregations merged and voted to recall him as pastor of the merged congregation.

I flew to Winston-Salem representing two causes: to invite Ed to return as pastor and to ask Helen to become editor of *Words of Cheer* and the new publication that was to replace it as well as to return to *Christian Living*. It was a delicate maneuver: the success of the operation called for a four-way correlation. But all parties agreed, so Helen became editor of *Words of Cheer* effective with the September 20, 1970 issue.

So one half-time assignment was now in place. What about *Purpose* and the half-time news editor for *Gospel Herald*?

At the suggestion of former executive editor Ellrose Zook, I contacted David Hostetler, a former missionary to Brazil, now a student in religious journalism at Syracuse University. He and his wife Rosanna had five children, and he was a little surprised at the small salary I was able to offer. But he accepted and his name first appeared as news editor of the *Gospel Herald* on July 27, 1971. In *Purpose* we find his name as editor starting October 10, 1971.

My memories of preparing the annual budget are less than pleasant. A majority of persons in the division divided their time between more than one periodical. Yet each periodical required a unified budget. I might be asked to combine one-fourth of a secretary's time at a secretary's rate of pay with one-half of an editor's time at an editor's rate along with various other costs which accrued to the publication.

Like the character in the old cartoon "Born thirty years too soon," I was caught with primitive technology. I would borrow an ancient mechanical machine no longer used by the accounting department and struggle my way through the process. In later years, computer accounting came in and my last several budgets were not so bad. But the early ones were painful.

I have reviewed the annual reports for the period of the Periodical Division and find them overly preoccupied with two issues: circulation and finances. Of course, these were aspects of the work which could be readily objectified for inclusion in such a report.

Ben Cutrell had determined that the book and congregational literature divisions should have promotion managers but that periodical editors should do their own circulation promotion. At first we rather welcomed this—to have the destinies of our publications under our full control. But as time went on and circulations sagged, there was some feeling of resentment, as if we were considered less important than those with more resources.

In his first annual report on behalf of this new division, Ben wrote, "Declining circulation gives us concern. We are constantly reviewing the factors involved and want to be alert to those we can control." The circulation report which followed showed each of the periodicals with declining circulation.[71]

I took the position that each editor should do *some* circulation promotion. We also engaged occasional consultants to advise or direct our circulation efforts. In the long run it was a losing battle. At the end of the Periodical Division's existence the circulation of all periodicals was less than at the beginning. And yet as I write, all are yet being published except for *Gospel Herald,* which merged with another publication.

A frank response from a non-renewing *Christian Living* reader gave one perspective: "We simply have too many periodicals and getting through them was an unacceptable burden. *Christian Living* had become less priority reading than *Gospel Herald, Sojourners, Festival Quarterly,* and even *Organic Gardening.*" Another said, "We enjoy *Christian Living* . . . but to cut down the cost, we will be sharing it with a friend."

In his 1972 report Ben Cutrell wrote, "I have been telling our periodical editors that they should not measure their effectiveness entirely by circulation figures. We do enjoy a high degree of saturation in our church membership. *Christian Living* must be promoted intensely to individual or family buyers. The other magazines are bought primarily by congregations or groups. . . . I am committed to a reasonable market penetration and non-growth if we can balance our expenses and income."[72]

One way to respond to static or declining circulation was to raise prices more than inflation. Another was to look for cost reduction strategies. *Gospel Herald* and *Christian Living* had the number of their pages reduced and *With* reduced the number of yearly issues. To save postage we began to mail the weekly publications *Purpose* and *On the Line* in monthly packets as was already being done with *Story Friends*.

Two years later David Hostetler reconfigured the design of *Purpose*. It had come to us as a twelve-page horizontal publication. This distinctive shape set it off from other periodicals, but added to the printing costs. Dave redesigned it as an eight-page vertical. The new size could be printed more efficiently, saved paper, and called for less editorial material. I am not aware that we received any complaints about the change, and we saved $4,488 in printing costs the first year.[73]

In the 1982-1983 report I wrote that "the last year has been touched by irony; though circulation of our publications continues to decline, we have earned more division income in actual dollars than ever before."[74]

As division director I looked for ways to provide intellectual stimulation. There developed among us periodical editors a practice of eating lunch together at a local restaurant once a week. This perhaps showed mild rebellion against the MPH practice of a thirty-minute lunch. Since we were all on salaries there was no good reason why we had to be back in the building by 12:30 p.m. But because we were a group our goings and comings were no doubt noticed by persons whose assignments kept them to their desks.

This luncheon provided an opportunity to exchange professional and other information, and I used it as an occasion to make announcements. After some years I got the impression that Ben Cutrell was not entirely pleased with this practice and I changed to a breakfast meeting, but it seemed as if something was lost. We also had occasional one-day seminars at the nearby Laurelville Mennonite Church Center.

In the meantime recruitment responsibilities kept turning up. In 1972, only about two years into the new division, John Drescher indicated his intention to resign as editor of *Gospel Herald.* Ben Cutrell took John and me out to lunch and tried to persuade him to continue as editor. But it was as if a buzzer had gone off in John's mind to tell him the time had come. He did not rush away, so we had time to look for a replacement.

In his 1972 report Ben wrote that John's resignation "has created some anxiety among the readers and with those of us responsible to find his replacement. The good job John was doing will be difficult to match." The publication board appointed Rufus Jutzi, Arnold Roth, and Ben Cutrell as a committee "to recommend a new editor to the Board."[75] Later Ben assigned me to his place on the committee and we worked at compiling a list of candidates.

Some time after this the other members of the committee began to look at me as a candidate for this assignment. I was not quite sure what to think about it. One day I would think "yes" and another day "no." I was aware that numbers of people in the churches took the *Gospel Herald* more seriously than any of the other periodicals. On the other hand, I rather liked the relative freedom of *Christian Living,* where the staff could make their plans without feeling responsible to report the work of denominational agencies.

In the end I did agree to accept the assignment. I expected that additional staff time would be allotted in light of my administrative work—a full time news editor perhaps—but this would come only years later. So I changed from a monthly to a weekly deadline, a change that took some adjustment. I discovered, however, that it was possible to speed up a weekly schedule if something important loomed in the future.

Accepting a new assignment for myself meant that I now had the task of finding someone to take my place as *Christian Living* editor. The idea emerged to offer this to J. Lorne Peachey, founding editor of *With*, a publication for teenagers. After five years, would he like a change? Having been somewhat involved with group dynamics I reasoned that he might want to help discern whether he should move. He replied that if I wanted him to edit *Christian Living* I should ask him to do it! So I did and he accepted.

His introduction as the new editor reported that Lorne was a graduate of the Syracuse (N.Y.) University School of Journalism and had been editor of *With* since 1968. It noted also that he had served *Christian Living* as a student intern in summer 1960 and as assistant editor from 1964-1969. He had taught at Western Mennonite School, Salem, Oregon, from 1961-1964.[76]

So the next move was to find someone to replace Lorne as *With* editor. We found Richard Kauffman, graduate of Eastern Baptist Theological Seminary and Temple Universit, and pulled him from work as editor of the *Franconia Mennonite Conference News* and Franconia Nurture Commission executive secretary. As he looked forward to the assignment, Dick wrote, "My primary concern is helping readers sort out what it means to be a disciple of Jesus in a complex society where there are many alternate lifestyles and philosophies."[77]

For several years we worked into our new assignments, then the scene changed again. In 1976 Alice Hershberger, editor of *Story Friends* came down with cancer. Marjorie Waybill, trained as an elementary school teacher, offered to substitute for Alice. Marjorie has recalled that after hearing of Alice's illness, "I couldn't sleep that night as I thought of Alice." She later called me at home, so no one at MPH would hear me, and confided that "if they were planning to look for an editor to help Alice I would be interested."

We were interested, so we asked Marjorie to cover for *Story Friends* until Alice could do it again. But Alice died and Marjorie edited *Story Friends* until her retirement in 1996. Marjorie recalled that division secretary Roxie Yoder introduced her to the task. "She explained how to buy stories, activities, and photos. She showed me how to submit copy to production, how to prepare art orders, and what to keep in mind as I chose the second color for the month. . . . It was Roxie who trained me, because by the time I took over, Alice was too ill to provide much help."

Reviewing the annual reports again, I find that although circulation and finances are prominent, we were at work on broader bases as well. For example, the 1977-1978 *Annual Report* mentions two special efforts of the division. One was a "self study of some principles involved in writing and editing." Each editor was assigned one of these principles and led in a discussion of that topic. The other was a consultation with writers held June 25-28 at Laurelville Mennonite Church Center, with about one-third of the expense covered by a grant from the Schowalter Foundation. Each editor was encouraged to invite five writers to the consultation.[78]

Among the assignments I gave to editors was a one-hour presentation on "Fiction for Children" by Marjorie Waybill. She has reported that she wrote me a memo indicating she could not do it. But, she says, I "simply wrote back saying 'You will present from 9-10 on Wednesday.' She recalls, "That was the most difficult assignment I had faced as an editor up to that time. I remember writing to different friends requesting prayer for my preparation and presentation. The presentation went well and I thanked God for the prayers of my friends and the confidence my supervisor had in me."

The inflation of the 1970s kept us scrambling. In 1983-1984 I wrote "to illustrate the cumulative effect of inflation, one can observe that the *Gospel Herald* cost $6.75 per year in 1973 when I became editor. It is now $18.95, an increase of 181%." In that same year all of our periodicals lost circulation but four of the six produced a margin of income.[79]

If I were to run this race again (which of course I cannot) I think I would concentrate specifically on seeking to make those six publications as efficient and as available as possible. This was our main mission, but occasionally we made an effort to start another publication. The efforts were perhaps noble but in the end not much came of them.

The closest to come to fruition was the attempt to begin a newsletter for older persons. Lorne Peachey developed a prospectus for the newsletter and made contacts in four Mennonite communities to test it. He concluded that a pilot issue was needed to give people a better idea of whether they would want such a publication. I applied for a $5,000 grant from Mennonite Mutual Aid to cover the cost of the pilot issue. We received the grant but in February, 1980, Mennonite Publication Board rejected our proposal to develop a pilot issue.

Since we already had the money, MMA allowed us to use it to prepare a special issue of *Christian Living* devoted to the subject of aging. This special issue appeared as March-April 1983, and copies were sent to all congregations of the Mennonite Church, Mennonite Brethren, Brethren in Christ, General Conference Mennonite, and Evangelical Mennonite Church, followed by a promotional campaign. The journalistic quality of the special issue illustrated what can be done when adequate resources are available.[80]

Another project that interested us was the possibility of publishing a theological journal. In 1978 I reported that Richard Kauffman was working on a prospectus for such a publication. We were well aware of *Mennonite Quarterly Review* but found its narrow focus seeming to allow for us to raise the question, "Where can Mennonite scholars have conversation about the implications of the Anabaptist tradition for a broad range of scholarly topics?" We thought the editor could be a member of the scholarly community with a managing editor at Scottdale. Richard found "some interest" and I applied for a grant from the Schowalter Foundation to support additional development. We did not receive the grant and eventually gave up on a theological journal. Meanwhile Conrad Grebel College began to publish *Conrad Grebel Review* in 1983.

The situation raised the question of our ability to develop and publish this sort of journal. Did we have the status and resources to do it? The answer seemed to be "no." It was as if the torch of theological leadership had gone away from Scottdale. In the early decades of the century, when Daniel Kauffman was chief theological articulator for the church, many roads (particularly railroads) led to Scottdale. But in our time we could not expect to provide the same level of theological leadership. Educational institutions were better situated to do this. It seemed it was better for us to work at theological popularization and let the higher level intellectualizing be done in academic settings.

Also educational institutions had access to funds we knew not of. While it is generally assumed that schools will not survive on tuition alone, Mennonite Publishing House could only cover the costs of "money losers" from "money makers" and had to be cautious about experimenting. After I retired I noted that MPH employed a fund raiser for a time, but I am not clear how well that experiment succeeded.

Another issue that got our attention was the idea of a publication for thirteen- and fourteen-year-olds. This is a special age, we were told, and these young people needed a publication to speak to their specific place in life. We did not doubt this, but we faced the problem of cutting into the markets for publications such as *On the Line* and *With*. I assigned Dave Graybill to study the question. Dave was familiar with our system, having served temporarily with *Christian Living, Purpose,* and *Gospel Herald* while various editors were on leave. Dave set up some focus groups to address the question. The result of his study did not support a new publication.

In my 1978 report I likened an editor to "the scribe . . . trained for the kingdom of heaven . . . who brings out of his treasure what is new and what is old." (Matt. 13:52.) I suggested that "The editor must be well grounded in the tradition, must know the denominational shibboleths, must have a concern for the people to be served. Yet it is not enough to articulate only what has been said for generations or what readers themselves would have thought about. There needs to be something more. To obtain this something more, editors need to read, study, travel, and in other ways gain stimulating experiences."[81] Editorial efforts to gain stimulating experiences are reported from time to time.

In fall 1977 David Hostetler attended the University of Pittsburgh. J. Lorne Peachey and Richard Kauffman assisted with news editing for the *Gospel Herald* during his half-time leave.[82] In 1978-1979 J. Lorne Peachey studied at Goshen Biblical Seminary and Dave Graybill served as *Christian Living* assistant editor in Lorne's absence.[83] Richard Kauffman spent the 1980-1981 year at Princeton Theological Seminary. He continued to edit *With* magazine and Lorne Peachey designed the publication.[84]

All of these assignments were carried out as study leaves. I myself arranged for a sabbatical in 1979-1980. Mennonite Publishing House had developed a sabbatical policy but only two persons had to this point made use of it: personnel director Nelson Waybill in 1966 and publisher Ben Cutrell in 1976. I applied for and was granted an eight-month reprieve from editing the *Gospel Herald.*

During the first four months I continued administrative work and prepared the budgets for the next year. During this time I took two courses at Pittsburgh Theological Seminary.

Then I cut loose altogether, and Mary and I took a 13,000 mile trip around the border of the country.

We visited Mennonite congregations and prepared congregational "profiles" for a book I entitled *From Germantown to Steinbach* (Herald Press, 1981). These were the names of the Mennonite churches at the beginning and end of the trip. Mary wanted to call the book *A Mennonite Odyssey* and I should have listened to my wife. The title I gave it sounded too much like an "ethnic" piece. I had deliberately tried to avoid ethnicism by including congregations of various Mennonite groups and ethnic backgrounds.

The book did not sell well, although it got a positive review by John A. Lapp in *Mennonite Weekly Review* and occasional other positive responses.[85] But at least Mary and I were able to take the expenses of the trip as an income tax deduction. Also, I found later that leftover copies could serve as gifts for new *Gospel Herald* subscribers. And once in awhile I have met a person who has discovered the book and read it with appreciation.

Some time after this I began to toy with the idea of resigning as administrator of the Periodical Division. I have on hand a copy of an undated memo directed to Mary, Ben Cutrell, and myself in which I reviewed some aspects of the assignment and asked whether it was time to cut back on my administrative work and concentrate on *Gospel Herald*. There is no date on the memo but it was evidently written in the early 1980s.

I expected that some younger person might become division administrator. What happened instead was that four of the six publications were transferred to the Congregational Literature Division while *Christian Living* and *Gospel Herald* continued as the Periodical Division. This change is first apparent in the *1984-85 Annual Report* where it is announced that although both publications had lost circulation, both increased their operating income for a total increase of more than $15,000.[86]

There was considerable personnel turnover that year also. J. Lorne Peachey resigned to become a designer and manager of a credit union. Richard Kauffman transferred to Goshen Biblical Seminary. David Hostetler became editor of *Christian Living,* and Steve Shenk came on as managing editor of *Gospel Herald,* a full-time assignment. So now I had more time to devote to the work of *Gospel Herald.*

In 1988 J. Robert Ramer became the new publisher and discerned that there were more persons reporting to him than he preferred. Among other changes Ramer made was to fold the remaining publications of the Periodical Division into the Congregational Literature Division. So after prividing the institutional context within which for eighteen years MPH periodicals were produced, the Periodical Division ceased to exist, although all the publications continued. To the readers of our publications such a change probably meant little or nothing. To recount it may be more for my own sake than for anyone else. But eighteen years of effort had gone into the attempts to nurture it.

As I began work on this chapter I sent notes to former members of the division for any comments they might have about our experience. I have already quoted Marjorie Waybill above. Another memory of Marjorie's was of how she and Roxie Yoder worked together on a special promotion campaign for *Story Friends.* They prepared a special issue of the magazine and had extra copies printed to send them to those congregations not subscribing. When Roxie went to mail them it was discovered that the extra copies had been shredded as surplus. Marjorie remembered "I cried all the way home that evening."

John Drescher recalled, "What strikes me now is how autonomous we really were. Except for a meeting now and then it seems we did our own thing." David Hostetler was not about to protest this state of affairs; he liked it that way. "One of the things we editors could count on was the freedom to do our work to the best of our abilities without having someone look over our shoulders."

Helen Alderfer commented "I thought our division was the best in MPH. And my office was the best. Once after a school class had been in for a demonstration of *On the Line*, the last boy out backed up, looked in, and said, 'It's neat in here.'"

Secretary Elva Yoder who spent twenty-five years with the *Gospel Herald* recalled the work with pleasure. "I found it to be interesting and fulfilling. I enjoyed learning what was going on in the church and learning to know many of its leaders."

The late Roxie Yoder served as division secretary from 1971 to 1989. Roxie was a positive person although she lived with constant pain. In spring 1989 she announced her decision to retire but added, "In doing this I realize I am giving up the best job at MPH." With a secretary like this in the division some good things had to happen.

Since the closing of the Periodical Division was simply an organizational change one should not take it too seriously. But its passing provides an occasion to reflect on the significance of literature for the Mennonite Church.

Barbara Wheeler, Auburn Theological Seminary president, reported recently on a study she made of an evangelical seminary and commented in general on the American evangelical "culture" in contrast with that of the so-called "mainline" churches. She is impressed by the way evangelicals carry Bibles to churches and some even have special covers for them. By contrast, she writes, "mainline Protestants do not handle much of anything. . . . A religious tradition that has little or nothing to look at, listen to, and touch cannot sustain us very long."[87]

Where to place Mennonites among American religious groups is a question for discernment. We have some cherished beliefs that readily connect with few or any other traditions. How to illuminate and pass on these convictions is a task not to be taken lightly. If we had thought about it, we would have seen our periodicals providing something for people to look at and touch. As communication methods change it will be worthwhile to consider in what ways the church can continue to provide objects for people to "look at, listen to, and touch."

9

Building Consensus

One day in the mid-seventies, David Hostetler and I were traveling in a car with C. Norman Kraus, a professor at Goshen College. He asked me what we saw ourselves "doing" in *Gospel Herald*. With no time for a studied response I said, "Building consensus."

A week or two later I met a man in Florida who asked the same question. I gave the same answer, but it did not seem to work as well. Someone was waiting to take me to the airport and there was not time to explore his concern adequately. But as near as I could tell, he saw "consensus" as a concept which lacked proper authority. As if a group got together and began talking: consensus would be whatever came out of the meeting.

With a little more time I believe I could have come up with a more satisfactory term. "Building conviction" perhaps. As I have reviewed the *Herald* for the period when I was editor, I find regular expressions of conviction: my own and others'.

The makeup of the magazine when I began as editor included several distinct elements. It may be that how each contributed to building consensus or conviction was not immediately apparent. There was a section of magazine articles, a news section, a report of births, marriages and obituaries, a religious news page and an editorial. Also letters to the editor. I introduced a column devoted to statements of opinion which I labeled "Hear! Hear!" It was my assumption that such statements need not be based on the sort of documentation expected in a regular article. The difference may not have been obvious. On occasion it appeared that to be placed in this column conveyed to the author that the communication was assigned a lower status.

I came to the *Herald* from editorial assignments where there was more time to brood over material before it was published. *Gospel Herald* editors were not privileged to brood for very long. Get it written. Get it edited. Send it to the printers.

In line with their penchant for lengthening the process, the printers asked for some material earlier than others. We supplied two separate dummies (that is a mockup of how the material should look when printed). We submitted an article dummy ten days before mailing time and a news dummy a week later. To keep it as current as possible, the editorial went in with the news dummy.

We did not spend much time in editorial consultation. The news editor was responsible for the news stories; the secretary compiled the census data; and I organized the articles, selected the world religious news, edited the letters and generally wrote the editorial. Although there was no time for delay, we did substitute for each other during vacation or sickness.

Much of the news came to us unasked. Church institutions, particularly, had perceived the need to get the word out and had developed information offices. Increasingly, semi-official groups sensed the value of putting their best foot into the news stream. Although our schedules were tight, I took the position that we ourselves should do some reporting. We thus planned to "cover" all meetings of the Mennonite Church General Board and one meeting a year of each of the five Mennonite Church program boards. Beyond this we basically relied on news sent to us.

From time to time we editorialized on the subject of church news. On December 7, 1976, news editor David E.

Hostetler published an editorial on "What Makes Church News?" He observed that "Ideally, church news should be the recording of God's action among us and our response to that action." But, he added, "It is not always easy to determine what God is doing through his people in the world." Also, "The question of significance becomes important."

He noted further that the most important news happens in congregations, but we have had limited success in getting news from congregations. He acknowledged that the large majority of our news was coming from official church institutions. "We may have a disproportionate amount of information from these organizations in comparison with that from congregations or districts."

He recognized also that most of the news from these organizations was good news and that "stories of poor decisions or failures are sometimes omitted [to keep people from losing confidence in the institutions] and to avoid hurting those involved." He noted further that "there are questions as to how much bad news [readers] really want to hear." Yet he ended the editorial by affirming our "goal to carry all the news necessary for your understanding of how the church is functioning, whether good or bad."[88]

This editorial summarized nicely the tension we lived with. Our publication's limited resources meant we needed to depend heavily on material prepared by the organizations themselves. Much of the time this was satisfactory. We worked in a small family style denomination where there were various networks of relationships and sources of information. And we considered the agencies our fellows in the faith and in the church. But once in awhile we wanted to assert our journalistic independence and report a happening which the institution would have preferred to keep quiet.

An example was "Two EMC Music Teachers Resign" which appeared on January 11, 1977. This was based in part on a report in the student newspaper *The Weather Vane*. It appeared as a minor story in an issue which contained a special section on Mennonite education and an editorial which wrote affirmatively about the relation between the church and its colleges.

The story alarmed college administrators. They wondered if this was a new policy in news reporting. We tried to be reassuring but firm. David Hostetler wrote to President Myron Augsburger, reminding him that the story was already out in *The Weather Vane* and that this was really no new policy. He noted further that "some of our more perceptive readers are calling for more than routine institutional information."

A complicating factor was that David had interviewed the president by phone concerning the issue. Since David had a son in the college, Myron had assumed he was talking to a patron and was dismayed to discover that his comments about the issue became news. So the president wrote to me also. I responded that "The *Gospel Herald* erred in not making clear to you that you were being interviewed for publication." I concluded with the pious hope "that all of us who are accountable to the Mennonite Church can operate in a way that builds trust among us and with the church." My letter indicates that I sent copies to five other Mennonite college administrators.

At least one *Gospel Herald* reader was glad for the story. Paul W. Shank of Goshen, Indiana, wrote, "I appreciate the candor of the explanation on the reasons behind the resignations. I hope the same approach will be followed in other church news so we don't need to read a report and then wonder what really happened."[89]

More often the concerns represented nuances, different interpretations of what happened at a meeting. An April 23, 1985 news story highlighted the work of a sexuality committee. The Mennonite Church General Board had brought the chair of this committee from Waterloo, Ontario, to Denver, Colorado, for a progress report. I led off my news story with the work of this committee.

I find as I review my article that I sought to follow the principle of "significance" mentioned by David Hostetler. Indeed two-thirds of the space is given to consideration of the committee's document "Human Sexuality in the Christian Life." I justified this emphasis at the beginning of the story when I wrote, "Judged by the volume of notes I have, sexuality was one of the most urgent topics discussed by the Mennonite Church General Board at its spring meeting."

As an effort to cover my tracks I mentioned that "Other important topics too numerous to report in detail were discussed and/or acted on in its two-day session." Then I reported several of them. But in terms of space, sexuality received the most emphasis.[90]

General Secretary Ivan Kauffmann was troubled by my emphasis. He wrote, "I felt that the discussion on the Human Sexuality document was given more than its share of space. . . . I also feel that it didn't deserve the headline. A reader can easily get the impression that General Board spent over half its time on this particular issue. Does the dramatic and controversial item deserve that much attention?"

In response I wrote, "We do not have the space nor the reader, the patience to report everything that happens at a board meeting. Also as a reporter I try to find a dominant theme or an interesting topic. For what other topic at the Denver meeting did the board fly a committee chairman from Waterloo to Denver to discuss the report?"

As a publication for the Mennonite Church, we assumed that the *Gospel Herald* should take seriously the biennial sessions of the Mennonite Church General Assembly. How to do this did not become clear to me right away. It was assumed that the news editor would write a quick review of the meeting and publish it as soon as possible.

But I had a feeling that something more should be done. In 1975, I wrote a more extended reflection on the assembly and published it several weeks later.[91] So there were two reports. In 1977, I drafted other members of the Periodical Division to help with the reporting. Finally in 1981 it occurred to me to assign to the news editor the organizing and editing of the coverage of the assembly (it was news after all) and this seemed to work better. This biennial special issue became a major activity for us and we labored to get it into print as soon as possible, negotiating a special deadline with the printers.

I find as I review my editorials that I returned from time to time to the question of *Gospel Herald's* purpose and function. In 1978 I wrote, "The *Gospel Herald* functions by seeking to find and discuss our Mennonite agenda. What beliefs and activities do we have in common? Our editorial intention is to publish material in *Gospel Herald* because it is of Mennonite concern."[92] The same year I wrote, "Like periodicals in general, the *Gospel Herald* seeks to make a statement about what is discerned by the staff to be important *now*. By publishing every week, we keep a regular flow of news and comments about the Mennonite Church."[93]

In an editorial anticipating the seventy-fifth anniversary of the *Herald* in 1983 I wrote, "It is our understanding that the *Herald* is a publication for the whole church. It is not intended for special interests. The task of the *Herald* is to encourage unity and faithfulness. Or faithfulness and unity. Put it either way.

"Is this too big an order? Of course it is too big an order. But it is what has to be done."[94]

We took special notice of the passing of our seventy-fifth anniversary. We published both a special two-color issue on April 5, 1983 and a book entitled *Not by Might*, a sample of articles and editorials from the publication's seventy-five years along with profiles of the editors. Other members of the Periodical Division along with the publisher helped in the selection of materials to include in the book.

The title came from Zechariah 4:6b, which states that "Not by might, nor by power, but by my spirit, saith the Lord of hosts." After it had been selected the title was found with an editorial by former editor Paul Erb on March 13, 1951. "The great Messiah was a peasant of galilee," he wrote. "An obscure monk at Wittenberg sounded the note of the Reformation. A persecuted little group of Anabaptists brought into being the modern world separation of church and state. The Publishing House in which we write this editorial has grown in a few years from an attic press in a house down the street. God does not choose to work by the might of numbers."

Herald Press published the book but we did much of the marketing. When interest in purchasing the volume died down, we were able to use it in circulation promotion. When I retired there were still a few copies left.

As for the special issue, we published articles that gazed back on the Mennonite Church during the seventy-five years of our publishing, which looked at the present, and which sought to predict the future of our denomination. We also used the occasion to introduce a new typeface and a new design for the publication.

In the March 29 editorial which preceded this anniversary issue, entitled "Issues to think about," news editor David E. Hostetler wrote, "Our view of Christ as Lord must continue to emerge from a people dedicated to seeing him afresh every day in private devotions and regularly in common worship."

It was our ongoing concern.

In 1987 I asked, "So what are we trying to do in the *Gospel Herald*? To encourage faithfulness by the publication of news, opinion, and testimony. And to test the insights presented by publishing responses in 'Readers Say.' It is not a strict orderly process but we do it with the conviction that God may be praised even in our disagreements if our hearts are 'single' before him."[95]

What sort of articles should be published for this purpose? One of the first I commissioned was "Saving the Seventies." I gave the assignment to John E. Lapp, a bishop and patriarch in the eastern Pennsylvania Franconia Mennonite Conference. This was in 1973, the era of the first gasoline crunch in the U.S. and of the Nixon troubles. What would a Mennonite bishop write in response to such an assignment?

In good Mennonite fashion he went to the Bible and the Anabaptist tradition. As a text he used Ephesians 5:16, "redeeming the time, because the days are evil." He concluded, "To save the seventies will cost us some energy by way of personal self-denial. It can cost some pain and suffering to those of the brotherhood who will not become caught up in the cause. But it will certainly be a joyful event in the life of the total church as brothers and sisters together experience the newness of the attempts to save the seventies."[96]

If the rhetoric seems a little strong, we may remember that he and Mrs. Lapp contributed toward saving the 1970s and the years following by raising a large family, all of whom found places in the work of the church. At one time, the executive secretary of the general board, the executive secretary of Mennonite Central Committee, and the president of Eastern Mennonite College were all Lapp sons.[97]

Many articles came in without solicitation. Numbers of persons felt they had a message for our readers. Writing for the *Gospel Herald* could serve as a coming out for young pastors. I tried to take these submissions seriously, but was not always successful in giving them adequate attention. (If anyone whose article I neglected reads this, here is my confession.)

The problem was not new with me. I seem to remember that when I became editor, my predecessor John Drescher passed on to me a file of articles which he had not found a way to publish. And if I recall correctly, some of them had come to him from Paul Erb, the editor before him. In contrast, I recall on one occasion an article from Robert J. Baker, one of our more skilled writers. I read it and concluded that it was ready for publication with no editing. An editorial high point!

A program that provided some editorial resources and professional stimulation was dubbed "Meetinghouse." It had been the brain child of Maynard Shelly, one-time editor of *The Mennonite*. He had conceived it as a magazine insert such as *Parade* which appears in Sunday papers throughout the land.

This was found to be too elaborate, but what developed instead was a cooperative program between *The Mennonite* and the *Gospel Herald* for joint planning of certain articles and joint coverage of certain newsworthy events. Minutes of an initial planning session on May 25-26, 1972 (before I was editor) indicate the direction it was to go. The editors planned to schedule four joint Meetinghouse issues each year.

The first Meetinghouse issue was to "deal with the Anabaptist concept of evangelism in the context of the caring, sharing, community." The topic was chosen in the light of Key 73, an ecumenical evangelistic emphasis for 1973. As time went on the practice developed of scheduling article series or individual articles rather than special Meetinghouse issues.

We also expanded the scope of membership and activities. We received some grants which enabled us to conduct journalistic seminars and invite editors of official publications for other Mennonite groups. A picture taken at one of our seminars in 1974 includes editors of nine different Mennonite publications.[98]

Another source of editorial stimulation was membership in the Associated Church Press, a group of religious publications. It had begun as a Protestant group but as time went on some Catholic journals joined. Paul Erb had taken the *Gospel Herald* into the association and we continued the membership. The chief advantage was a once-a-year convention with speakers, seminars, and opportunities for "shop talk" with other editors.

The ACP sponsored an annual awards contest with judges who were not a part of our organization. So each year we editors would select materials form various categories of our publication and in most years we heard nothing from our submissions. But in 1985 I received the ACP Award of Merit for an editorial written during a period of staff turnover when I and the secretary were assembling the magazine without the help of an associate. The editorial, "Broken House, Broken Home?" appears as an appendix.

It was traditional for the editor of the *Gospel Herald* to travel. There is a persistent report that Daniel Kauffman, the first editor, served on twenty-two church-related committees. (I wonder how one would document this tradition.) Paul Erb told me once that he himself averaged one night a week on the train. John Drescher has written that "The job required me to be out in the church at least half the time."[99]

These men were revivalists and speakers at church-related events, roles already developed when they became editor. Since my background had been mainly editing, I was not widely perceived as a visiting speaker. When I traveled to a convention, I was more likely to write a report than to address the meeting.

I also participated quite regularly in the work of Allegheny Mennonite Conference along with certain denominational committee assignments. These included serving Goshen College as an overseer, 1966-1972, and as acting president, though not a member, of Mennonite Board of Education for a couple of years after that. I was a member of the committee which recommended Marlin Miller as president of Goshen Biblical Seminary beginning in 1975 and of the committee which recommended Victor Stoltzfus as president of Goshen College in 1984.

A committee assignment in the mid-1960s led to the drafting of a report which became a slim paperback book in 1971. A move surfaced to call for a Mennonite philosophy of education. It is my impression that initially it was expected to cover higher education only. But the study committee which emerged sought to represent all levels of church related education. I was appointed to represent Mennonite Publishing

House and ended up becoming chair of the research committee which was responsible to the study committee.

As chair of the research committee I found myself eventually drafting a report which was published as *Mennonite Education: Why and How?* (Herald Press, 1971).

In an introductory section entitled "Notes to the Reader in a Hurry." I included "6. *Our point of view.* We view the church as the people of God. . . . This special calling is both a privilege and a responsibility. Because their ultimate goals and manner of life will be different from others, the people of God have specific educational needs and problems." This was to be an effort to provide a philosophy of education for such a people.

It seems from this perspective a brash attempt. Albert J. Meyer, executive secretary of Mennonite Board of Education, critiqued it personally. Other members of the research committee basically went along with it. Although the philosophy was to apply to all our educational efforts, colleges were given special attention in that it was arranged for me to make presentations at Eastern Mennonite, Goshen, and Conrad Grebel colleges.

Informal feedback I received suggested that it may have been taken more seriously on the secondary level. Also it was understood that Herald Press published the book for our convenience and that we would purchase all the copies. But word got out, and there was sufficient interest to call for a second printing.

The book received brief notice in *Religious Education* magazine. It noted, "A committee statement of a philosophy of education, this little book reflects some of the current thinking in the field, but makes less use of interpersonal relations than one might expect (no Seabury or UCC types)."[100]

Occasionally I meet someone who remembers the book. The latest was a man I met in Calcutta, India, at the 1997 Mennonite World Conference. He confessed to having translated it for teaching he had done among, I think it was, Old Colony Mennonites in Bolivia. I was pleased to know he could use it.

The philosophy of education assignment was done before I became *Gospel Herald* editor in 1973. Before that date my role as an editor was less public than later. But invitations to undertake other public tasks continued. In 1980 Allegheny Mennonite Conference called. The call came from Edwin Alderfer, chair of the nominating committee while Mary and I were traveling in western Canada. He said they needed a nominee for moderator of the conference and had not found anyone else willing. Would I be willing?

Such appeals always impressed me. Indeed, if I could help to avert an emergency, why not do it? After returning home, I reviewed the option with publisher Ben Cutrell, and he was open to it. He saw it important for the editor of the *Gospel Herald* to be connected with the church. Since I had not circulated as a speaker in the manner of my predecessors, this made an opportunity for a connection.

So I consented and served as Allegheny moderator for four years in the early 1980s. The moderator's task was principally leading meetings, and this was something I could do if I had an agenda and a sense of what was expected to happen. I find on reflection that I have led a good many meetings on local, district, and churchwide levels. It has been intensive work but not impossible.

Yet it is an assignment not to be taken lightly. The leader of a meeting can never relax but always seek to anticipate the next development. I have been glad to do it, but I thought to myself after one intense meeting, *If I were to be damned, no fire would be needed. It would be punishment enough to go into the "ages of the ages" moderating a meeting.*

For several years I represented Allegheny Conference on the Mennonite Church General Board. This was a natural role for a district conference moderator, but it made me uncomfortable in the sense that as an editor I was an employee of a churchwide board while at the same time representing a regional conference. No one ever challenged my connection, and I endeavored to avoid taking advantage of it. For me the conflict became most obvious when the work of Mennonite Publication Board was being reviewed by the General Board. On that occasion I kept a low profile.

In the mid-1980s Allegheny Conference called again and persuaded me to take an assignment under a new system in which one served as moderator elect for two years followed by two as moderator. So I was involved for four more years and retired the same year as I retired as *Gospel Herald* editor.

All of this organizational activity was marginal to the main task, editing a weekly magazine. Although we always got it published, I am confident that some committee meetings cut into work that should have been done at home. Yet the change of pace served a purpose and the trips were enriching.

There were short trips and longer trips. I attended all the sessions of Mennonite World Conference after I became editor of the *Herald* and two of those before. I toured Israel in late winter 1974 and attended the congress on "World Evangelization" in Lausanne, Switzerland, the same year. In response to the former I wrote an editorial and for the latter I did a news report and a major illustrated feature.[101]

The next year I aspired to report on the assembly of the World Council of Churches in Nairobi, Kenya. Mary went with me and we visited Mennonite activities in Africa before, during and after the assembly: Ghana, Ethiopia, Kenya, Tanzania, Botswana, and Zambia. Mary took pictures and I wrote reports.[102]

In 1983 James Sauder, a missionary serving with Eastern Mennonite Missions, invited me to travel with him to Central America. I visited in three countries; Belize, Guatemala and Honduras, rubbing shoulders with missionaries and local church leaders.[103]

Three years later I represented Meetinghouse on a Central American study tour being sponsored by Mennonite Central Committee. Among countries we visited were El Salvador, Nicaragua, and Honduras.[104]

Finally in 1990 within months of my scheduled retirement, I was permitted a second trip to Israel. Instead of a tour this was a ten-day study session at Tantier, an ecumenical study center between Jerusalem and Bethlehem. As in Africa, I made contact with Mennonite activities in Israel and so enriched my experience in this small conflicted strip of real estate.[105]

All such experiences called for extra effort to prepare for the trip and to deal with the accumulated work upon return. But it was amazing how one could work a trip like this into a heavy schedule when one was determined to do so.

In 1983-1984 there was a major shakeup in *Gospel Herald* staff. David Hostetler resigned as news editor to become editor of *Christian Living*. Richard Kauffman replaced him but stayed only a few months. He left during the summer of 1984 to become a Goshen Biblical Seminary vice-president. So now I began a talent search. I settled on Steve Shenk, member of the information department at Mennonite Board of Missions. At this point I was allowed to employ a full-time person so I designated him managing editor and added to his news responsibility the assembly of the whole magazine issue by issue.

Steve began work in early October 1984 and has recalled a major step in his transition from information officer to editor. "As a PR person at MBM, I mailed a packet of news to the church press right before I left for Scottdale. A few days later, as an editor, I looked skeptically at the 'promotional' packet that landed on my desk. I was in a whole new role!"

But while we were skeptical of church agency news, we were not against our church agencies. For one thing, we could not afford to be. We did not have the resources to gather all the information they provided. More basically, we recognized that we and they were part of the same church organization and that the *Gospel Herald* was responsible to keep church members informed about what their institutions were doing.

In contrast to an independent publication which chose its field of interest and selected its readers, we inherited both through the Mennonite Church. We were indeed more independent than some church publications since Mennonite Publication Board was a separate church organization from the sponsors of these other agencies.

Yet I recognized that the stance of a church organization was delicate. It could not tax as the government does and although some activities had the benefit of endowments, most depended on voluntary contributions. I got the feeling that some agency people were disappointed that their news did not result in more direct support. I recall that on one occasion we reported the need for money to support a program of Bible correspondence lessons for prisoners. Money promptly flowed in, and I gathered that some wondered why we could not do that for them more regularly.

Gospel Herald was a more reader-responsive magazine than others I had edited before. As a curriculum editor I seldom heard from readers unless they found problems with the material. With *Christian Living* reader response was somewhat sporadic. *Gospel Herald* was different. Among the readers were those who felt a need to commend or condemn published material. "Readers Say" had been introduced by Paul Erb, second editor of the publication. Daniel Kauffman, the first editor, was evidently not comfortable with this public display of reader response. George R. Smoker, who served with Kauffman as office editor for a time recalled to me that he had introduced a column of letters labeled "Open Forum" while Kauffman was ill and not in the office. "It made him get well pretty fast," recalled Smoker. Indeed, this column seems to have appeared only twice; July 31, and August 21, 1941.[106]

After Paul Erb, letters to the editors were a regular feature in the publication. Because I perceived my time as short I did not spend much time editing the letters. Generally I did not answer them but printed them promptly and let this serve as a sign to the readers that they were being heard.

Looking back, however, I can see that a little more studied consideration of the letters and their place in the *Herald* could have been helpful. As I reviewed them, numbers of the letters seemed too long and certain writers appeared over and over. I am told that letter writers are a type—and I write an occasional letter to an editor myself. Letter writers have a more than average desire to set the world straight. Writing to an editor and being published gives them a sense of accomplishment. At least they got one editor's attention!

On occasion during my seventeen years as editor of *Gospel Herald*, I told myself that because of the public nature of this assignment, I should retire at sixty-five. I was a little surprised to find that the publisher had the same idea. No doubt if he had asked me to continue for a year or two longer I would have been flattered to think that my services were that urgent. As it happened, my successor was waiting in the wings, and I retired on my sixty-fifth birthday.

There was some trauma connected with retiring after thirty-eight years with the same institution. The most obvious was the loss of a work station. MPH, probably wisely, does not provide space for retired persons. The first time I entered the building after retirement, I felt like an interloper.

But I was allowed to keep a key so I can use the library after regular office hours. In contrast to first editor Daniel Kauffman, who lived only weeks after he retired, I have been young enough to explore a variety of interests and respond to numbers of invitations. There is life after editing.

10

Having Written

Addressing a Mennonite writers' conference in the mid-1950s, Kenneth Wilson, editor of *Christian Herald* magazine, noted that "Many people would like to have written." At this point in my life I am on the other half of that dilemma. I have written something less than 1,000 editorials. To write them was sometimes difficult, but no impossible chore.

What is the ongoing significance of all these editorials? It occurred to me to go back and review the whole set to see what they appeared to be saying.

The first editorial I wrote after arriving in Scottdale was for *The Mennonite Community* magazine and appeared in January, 1953. The last was for the *Gospel Herald* of October 3, 1990. In between I wrote editorials also for *Christian Living* and *Builder* magazines.

Although as office editor of *The Mennonite Community* my chief responsibility was to assemble the monthly issues and work with the printers in the production of the magazine, I find editorials of mine in eight of the twelve 1953 issues. Evidently the committee of editors welcomed my participation with them in the monthly editorializing. (Typically each issue carried two editorials.) I copied two of these eight editorials for closer examination. What seemed to motivate this writer?

It appears that these two editorials follow the direction of "wisdom" as found in the biblical books of Proverbs and

Ecclesiastes. The writer assumed that there is a better way and we ought to choose it. Certain assumptions are stated and the editorial reasoning follows them.

"A Little Money, a Little Time" (June 1953) proposes that while Americans are much concerned about money, we are short of time. It indicates that there are other cultures less concerned about money, but they have more time. The editorial proposes that "There is the possibility of a middle course." This middle course is highlighted by the title and suggestions one offered for some things to do with the combination.

What about this middle way? Is it really a little left of center? Nothing very radical here. Just the sensible musings of a twenty-seven-year-old who had grown up on a hard-scrabble farm in eastern Pennsylvania. But with parental support and the relative affluence of World War II and the post-war years, he had been able to finish five years of higher education debt free. There is a "can do" tone in the editorial. "With a little money you can buy the essentials," I wrote. "With a little time you can enjoy them."

A second editorial, "As One who Serves" (December) has a sharper edge. It takes off from the teaching of Jesus which surprised his disciples, "the idea that greatness lies in service." The editorial proposes further that "The Christian who would surprise his non-Christian neighbors may do so by living among them as one who serves." No doubt the young adult naiveté of one who has seldom met greediness head on. Yet there is a kind of wisdom here, and among us the Source cannot be gainsaid.

From the issue of January 1954 through March 1960 I did not write editorials. I was busy enough with my work as assistant editor of *Christian Living* and also wrote a number of articles for the magazine. Editorializing for *Christian Living* was chiefly the work of the editor, Millard Lind. In February 1960 he resigned; my first *Christian Living* editorial appeared in April that year.

Now it is the editor writing, not just an office editor, and there is a tradition to support. The first editorial, entitled "Business as Usual" affirms that "we want to continue in the pattern set during the past six years." It quotes from Millard Lind's first editorial, "Something Old and Something New." As implied by Lind's title, this was that as the world changes, the old responses must find new faces. So my editorial calls for change and adaptation to a changing world with a clincher from 2 Corinthians 3:18, "changed into the same image from glory to glory, even as by the Spirit of God." It was a theme to appear over and over during the years of my editorializing.

My final 1960 editorial was entitled "Something New at Christmas" and gave the old/new theme a little different twist. It acknowledged the mixture of Christmas traditions, some with a decidedly pagan background. But it expressed the opinion that even such an old holiday can include an expression of newness. "A great deal of thinking about Christmas is of the old variety," I wrote. "But here and there the new breaks through, for the celebration is in honor of the newness of the gospel." Perhaps a little left of center?

And so as the months and the years rolled on there would be repetition of these themes with variations. In January 1964 I wrote "Face Forward," an editorial which included the statement that "Continual gazing backward will not alter the fact that certain crucial change points have been passed." In June I wrote that "Truth is not so much a place to stand as a way to go."

In October of that year I wrote the first of a good many editorials on ecology. I believe I saw concern for ecology as a recognition that our resources come from God and thus should be used responsibly. I wrote "As with the conservation of the soil, the need for clean air and pure water is closely related to the conservation of human life and community living." I fear this idea was not original with me and that I should have given credit for it to Silas J. Smucker, who published two articles on conservation in *The Mennonite Community*, February and April 1951.

In June 1966 there is the first editorial related to auto safety. In March 1967 I shared a statement of faith: "Our Point of View." Among other beliefs, I wrote, "We believe . . . the Christian way is a pilgrimage." No new thought for me, surely.

In March 1973 I addressed an open letter to Norman Vincent Peale taking him to task for the easygoing patriotism I found in a tract he had published. In May I wrote against the use of alcoholic beverages and in June I wrote that "Jesus on the cross was more powerful in the long run than Pilate and the priests who put him there. Who follows in His Train?"

My final *Christian Living* editorial appeared in December 1973. Entitled "Summing Up," it cited and discussed four beliefs: 1) in Jesus Christ; 2) in love; 3) in freedom; 4) in work and play. It concluded that "Work and play in reasonable amounts give life balance and if done for Jesus' sake give it Christian meaning. Jesus, criticized for healing a man on the Sabbath, replied that His Father works all the time and He would too. An example, we do well to follow."

What did I mean by that? Certainly not to ignore the Christian sabbath. I think rather it was a concern not to be so tied down by rules that one is prevented from responding to needs that confront us and call for a non-traditional response.

In 1964 editorial direction of *Builder* magazine was added to my list of responsibilities. I was at that time heavily involved in a graduate educational program and not happy about this additional burden. For several nights I did not sleep well, but then I spent a few days away from Scottdale and my spirit revived. However, I did not write many editorials in *Builder* for the first several years.

But beginning in 1969 editorials appear regularly. *Builder* was intended as a publication for local congregational workers, a how-to-do-it for all persons with congregational responsibility. Some of these were better served than others, particularly Sunday school teachers and pastors. An editorial in February 1969, entitled "Why I Believe in Teaching the Bible" allowed me to address the issue of "a biblical point of view." I wrote that "One of the greatest tragedies of Bible study is that people may give their whole lives to it and still not understand this point of view."

In December 1970 I addressed the question "Is Worship Subversive?" I observed that "the people of God are like aliens, guerrillas. They live among a people with local loyalties and short range goals." I concluded that "Worship, then, is subversive in the sense that it substitutes the good news of God's love for the bad news of human pride and selfishness." The sense of division between church and world which informed my December 1953 editorial in *The Mennonite Community* was still with me. Was it perhaps first developed in the contrast I perceived between the etchings in the front of my grade school and the position of my church community?

A March 1972 editorial entitled "A Better Way" expressed in Christian educational terms a concern similar to what I had been writing since I began editorializing. "If there is one single message of *Builder* articles," I wrote, "it is the emphasis on a better way of doing our work, for God in the local congregation." I concluded with the words, "The secrets of the mystery of learning are only slowly unlocked. Yet this much we know: better learning comes in response to teachers who use the best methods they know. This is a better way."

My final *Builder* editorial appeared in June 1972 and concluded, "And so if I may be permitted one final exhortation it is this: the task is not to be taken lightly. It demands your best efforts and all the resources at your command. This is what *Builder* has been trying to say."

Well, of course. How could I have said any less?

One odd little happening stands out in my memories of *Builder*. We typically sold advertisements for the back cover, generally to some branch of Mennonite Publishing House. For

December 1969 we had no ad. What use should be made of this space?

It happened that there was a lesson on December 14 in the Uniform Bible Series based on the inter-testamental period. There were two biblical texts printed, Psalm 119: 1-8 and Luke 2:1-3, but obviously the inter-testamental period was one with which most Sunday school people were not familiar.

I discovered that Moody Institute of Science had produced a filmstrip entitled "Between the Testaments" and that Provident Bookstores at Lancaster, Pennsylvania and Kitchener, Ontario, had it for sale. I wrote a memorandum addressed to adult teachers and superintendents calling it to their attention. I have no documentation regarding the response, but I was told that it cleaned out all available copies of the filmstrip in these two stores and at Moody Institute of Science! How many copies there were I do not know. Perhaps only a few dozen. But on the surface it appeared to be the most effective ad I ever wrote.

In September 1973 I began as editor of *Gospel Herald*. For the next seventeen years, with one four-week leave in 1975 and an eight-month sabbatical in 1979-1980, I wrote an editorial nearly every week. This became a major part of my editorial work and I scheduled a special time for it—Thursday morning. Sometimes the writing went well and I was essentially finished by 10:00 o'clock. Other times it could take all day.

I had no grand design for editorial writing but addressed topics as they came to me. Sometimes they were related to trips I had made. At other times they addressed topics which surfaced in the magazine itself; again the subject grew out of my reading and I drew on a book as a resource. (A person once asked me whether I had to buy all of those books. "No," I replied, "I am on the library committee." Actually, I essentially was the library committee.)

The editorial process was always at work in the back of my mind. Topics would occur to me at any time, and I would make notes for later development. Sometimes when the time came for development, the topic did not look as useful as it first appeared. Also there were many times when Thursday morning came with no clear idea what to write. So it was necessary to say to myself, "Self. It's time to write. What are we going to do?" Something always came out.

I noticed when I went on sabbatical that I would get editorial ideas, then remember I was not then writing editorials. Eventually the ideas stopped coming and I began to worry about whether they would come again. Of course, a few weeks before the end of the sabbatical an idea came, so I was reassured the process still worked.

In a review of my 1973 *Gospel Herald* editorials, beginning with October 2, I find a new context but similar concerns. There is the necessary nod toward the tradition represented by the previous three editors. There is for me a new concern for the church organization. But there is the same sensitivity to the relationship between church and world. There is also ongoing emphasis on the need to perceive where we are in a changing scene.

In an October 16 editorial, "Why a Church Paper?" I wrote, "The *Gospel Herald* exists to help in discerning the signs of our times and the nature of the call to be God's people today." On October 30 I used John Howard Yoder's *The Politics of Jesus* as a source for an emphasis on the corporate nature of salvation. "The Christian alone is not a truly redeemed person," I wrote, "for salvation is the calling not so much of isolated persons as a people." Maybe this was a new detail in my thinking, but it fit well with what I had been writing as editor of *Christian Living*.

On November 20 I published "Going Back to Go Forward," with help from Alvin Toffler's three-year-old *Future Shock,* which I acknowledged that I had only recently found time to read. I responded to Toffler's challenges regarding things as they are and his effort to predict the future. But I found that some of Toffler's proposals for coping with change fit into what the church had been doing right along. "So there is no need for us to establish a new pattern, but rather to strengthen and breathe new life into those we have. One of the most common is the weekly gathering for worship and the celebration of life."

In "Violence and Deception," December 11, I commented on the U.S. Watergate experience and how much violence and deception are built into everyday experience. "A better method of dealing with one another has been shown by our Lord and his disciples."

Finally on December 25 I published "What Time is it at Christmas?" another effort to use the holiday for more than might meet the average eye. "What time is it at Christmas? Time to remember that we are God's people and that in Christ we have freedom to reorder our lives in line with His will and the opportunities open to us." Does it seem reminiscent of what I published in *The Mennonite Community* twenty years before?

Evidently these themes as I developed them were satisfactory to most readers of the *Gospel Herald*. In "Readers Say" there is only one entry during 1973 relating to an editorial and that response is positive. Indeed as I reviewed seventeen years of editorials I found no great outpouring of response to them. It was as if they were found generally satisfactory. As one writer put it on February 4, 1975, "I very much enjoy reading your editorials and would like to comment on the editorial 'Who is Yahweh?'

"Your subject is indeed an interesting study, yet I would that you had expanded further."

I returned again and again to themes of change and renewal. In "On Passing the Age of 50" (November 4, 1975) I wrote, "Age fifty is a time for renewal. In fact, it is there not the need and potential for renewal at any age? For even as the process of death begins at birth, so must renewal."

From time to time I commented on specific behavioral issues, particularly tobacco and alcohol. In "A Small Thing" (May 18, 1976) I wrote, "Is it a heavy burden that the church would lay upon us to ask the 90 percent who could handle alcohol to abstain for the 10 percent who cannot."

"I think not."

Response to this was basically positive but not completely so.

As in this editorial, what I wrote on occasion pinched someone. "A sense of Sadness" (June 6, 1977) was a critique of the life insurance system and drew pained responses from several insurance salesmen.

The ministry of women became a much-debated issue during the time I was editor, and I addressed the question from time to time. "Can a Woman Handle Money?" I asked on August 12, 1980. I responded that in 1 Corinthians 12 there is no indication that the spiritual gifts for the church are sex related. So I concluded, "Let us affirm the gifts He has assigned, whether female or male, and make use of them to the glory of God."

On January 29, 1985, I asked, "Would Paul have ordained Lydia had he known about ordination?" I made a similar point and supported a proposal brought to Allegheny Mennonite Conference "that congregations which desire to ordain women as leaders be permitted to do so, but this should not mean that everyone had to do it." I concluded, "In this as in other controversies, let us seek to learn the will of God as we are able. Let us then be respectful to others who disagree with us and continue to love and accept them." I am confident there were muttered protests to what I wrote, but the editorials seem not to have drawn written opposition.

I enjoyed writing about the interpretation of Scripture, particularly to call attention to its less noted aspects such as humor. In "Portrait of the Prophet as Bumbler" I held up the story of Jonah as an example of biblical humor. "It is assumed by many that the book of Jonah was written long after the time of its chief character, I wrote; "This was a good thing because no living person would take kindly to such ribbing." But I wrote that "if we will we may learn from [Jonah]. We may laugh at Jonah and when our laughter dies down we may recognize that we are laughing at our own rigidities."

The editorial troubled Clarence Fretz. His concern was compounded by the presence at the front of the issue of "Jonah: More than a Big Fish Story" an article by Gil Hellwig, which interpreted Jonah as a message to Israelites in the fourth century before Christ. Fretz wrote, "We have long given the *Gospel Herald* the honored place on a table in our living room. Will it continue to have such bold misinterpretations of the Scriptures on the front and back pages in the future? I hope not."

My concern was to have readers get a sense of the dynamic of Scripture. Why was this text written? What was its original purpose? I reasoned that if we got a sense of this we were in a better position to respond to its message for today. But it was a delicate process.

As I reflected on themes highlighted in this survey of editorials I asked myself whether I had neglected the great doctrines of the Christian faith. I believe in salvation by grace through faith, not of ourselves, but the gift of God. Did I say this or only assume it?

So I did a spot check and was somewhat reassured. I found, however, that references to doctrine were likely to be found in an editorial on another subject. This fits with my greater interest in biblical theology, history, and ethical issues than in systematic theology with its abstractions.

I found in "Faith and Forgiveness" on September 3, 1974, the statement, "One of the sharpest contrasts between the Christian faith and folk religion is in the area of faith and forgiveness. Folk religion has faith only in the efforts of man. The folk religionist may admit failure, but he never admits sin." (I am not sure who I had in mind as the "folk religionist," but clearly I did not agree.)

In "Easter Faith in the Epistles" (March 23, 1976) I wrote, "Though each of the books in the New Testament is an independent testimony, they have a common belief. This is that Jesus was the One sent by God. . . . They all are based on the common assumption that He died for our sins and was raised again."

On September 2, 1986, I asked, "Is there a Mennonite Spirituality?" I stated that "There have been and still are those who particularly stress the Christian's status as in 'Are you born again?' While not discounting the importance of personal repentance, a Mennonite spirituality cannot be satisfied with this alone. Mennonites must ask also, 'Are you following the Christian way?'" It was important to me to add that second element.

Because of my concern to treat the church as a separate entity my references to government tended to be negative or matter-of-fact. But after attending an activist minded peace conference I addressed an open letter to Ronald Reagan on July 6, 1982. I warned him that "peace people are starting to pray for you." I concluded the editorial with the words, "The short-cut methods of force and violence . . . can no longer be expected to work. The Bomb has made them obsolete. I dream of your becoming famous as the president who led the world toward a renunciation of these deadly weapons. Peace people are praying for miracles."

On September 14 we published a response from the White House: "You may be sure these views will receive careful consideration by this administration." The history of the world in the years since then indicate that the shortcut methods still prevail and that one should not expect great things from the political process. But people of faith must still pray.

As mentioned earlier, an issue to which I gave regular attention was the environment. On January 14, 1986, I asked, "Can we Live without the Tropical Rain Forests?" I wrote that "If it seems a petty thing to suggest that we ought not to eat hamburgers for the sake of a few bugs or flowers in a tropical rain forest, we might consider that the life of our grandchildren could be at stake as well. Think of that the next time you pull in at the golden arches." Whether anyone ever did do such thinking I never learned.

I felt so strongly about the environment that I wrote four environmental editorials during 1990, my final year with the *Herald*. In the last of these, "The Garden of God" (on October 23) I wrote, "I want to be remembered as one with a concern for the care of the earth. And I perceive that it is a biblical theme, though perhaps readily overlooked."

One of my final editorials "Life in the Colony of Heaven" appeared on October 16, 1990 and drew on the book *Resident Aliens* by Stanley Hauerwas and William Willimon. As implied in the title, their book takes as its theme Paul's statement in Philippians 3:20, "Our commonwealth is in heaven." Drawing on their imagery, I wrote that "Mennonites are at work on a new confession of faith. There may be those who expect any new confession of faith to be an erosion of Mennonite values. On the other hand, as Hauerwas and Willimon illustrate, a new statement from a fresh perspective may put the old values to work in the present and future in a manner the old statement could not do."

I couldn't have said it better!

So what was accomplished by all this editorializing? It occurs to me that editorials, like sermons and the evening news, are eminently forgettable. Perhaps this is as it should be. Although there have been times and cultures where people could remember just about everything, in our time we are so overwhelmed by data we also forget a lot to maintain our perspective.

Yet it is to be hoped that editorials, like sermons, will jog a memory, stick a pin in a conventional wisdom or event, or—can it be—change a behavior. To this preachers and editorial writers have dedicated their efforts.

11

After Editing

On occasion I meet acquaintances from editing days who wonders what I am doing. I find this halfway reassuring in that they consider it important to ask, but also a little annoying as if I am being called upon to justify myself. "I walk the dog," I sometimes begin, "keep a few bees and work in the garden." Then I move on to some of my church-related activities. It seems to reassure them to find I am not wasting away.

I have heard retired people say that they are busier after retirement than before. This seems to me a rationalization, but I should not speak for others. For myself, I observe that I am not as tightly disciplined as in the days when I arrived in the office soon after 7:00 and stayed perhaps until 4:30. If I am today not as efficient, I am surely not pushed as hard.

Having left a public assignment, I have the usual temptations to wonder whether I am still significant. And having grown up in a culture where I was expected to work to justify my presence, I am no doubt conditioned to work.

I have not viewed work as the curse implied in Genesis 3. Yes, of course there is drudgery in all work. Indeed there will be weeds in our gardens and details in every endeavor that detract from its efficiency. But when one perceives the end in view, a more productive garden or a properly functioning committee, one can accept the drudgery.

After I retired, I found that activities which had been marginal moved toward the center. Since editing no longer occupied the center, speaking or freelance writing could move in. The first big project I undertook after retirement was to go to Canberra, Australia, to report on the seventh assembly of the World Council of Churches. I had earlier covered the 1975 fifth assembly in Nairobi, Kenya. Although I had missed the 1983 sixth assembly in Vancouver, British Columbia, I continued an interest in the WCC because of my conviction that the church is international. In 1975 I had to work ahead and make special assignments to keep the *Gospel Herald* functioning while I was gone. Now I could simply get ready and go.

I wrote two articles on the WCC for the Meetinghouse group and also sent back a news report during the assembly. In the first article, written before I went, I considered why North American Mennonites are not members of the council. I reported that one congregation had canceled its *Gospel Herald* Every Home plan after I so much as featured the 1975 assembly. I suggested that our Mennonite suspicion of the WCC is part lack of information, part response to public propaganda, and part an instinctive concern about large bureaucratic organizations whose accountability is not clear to us. "At heart is possibly a different perspective on the relation between the churches and the political system."[107]

In a news report from the assembly I noted the presence of eight Mennonites and our sense that "there was much to affirm in the opening days of the assembly."[108] After it was over and I had time to reflect, I composed a third piece in which I tested the performance of the assembly against what I perceived as its vision and found it wanting.

I reported that on the last day of the assembly the WCC took a formal action against war and rescinded it after four hours. "This failure of the assembly to take a clear cut stand against war was disappointing," I wrote. "But the WCC is made up principally of establishment churches whose upper classes serve in governments and whose lower classes serve in armies and whose clergy wear vestments."

I concluded the article by reporting that John and Alice Lapp and I had left the assembly early and attended a meeting of the Mennonite fellowship in Sydney, Australia, which met in "Mark and Mary Hurst's living room." I suggested that the WCC way of doing church is "from above with bishops, archbishops, patriarchs, and official delegates who issue statements." I contrasted this with the Mennonite way: "To bring together a community of those who confess Christ and decide together that they want to follow him."[109]

I was a little uneasy with this neat comparison and acknowledged that the contrast was perhaps too simple and even judgmental. One *Gospel Herald* reader agreed with this. Julia Spicher Kasdorf, then of Brooklyn, New York, wrote, "Neither WCC or the Mennonite Church has realized its ideals. But to interpret the world through the frame of an idealized vision of one's own clan is unfair and dangerous. Yes, it is more comfortable to keep things within the family, but this is not wise or even possible. Such a defensive and ethnocentric stance is the last thing we need as our world grows smaller and the Mennonite Church grows increasingly diverse."[110]

She had a point! I had allowed myself the privilege of criticizing, and when we criticize another, we open the issue of of our own failures. Yet there was one detail which Julia had not perceived. She had apparently assumed that Mark and Mary Hurst were so-called "ethnic" Mennonites. In a letter published a few weeks later, Mark pointed out that he and Mary had not come from Mennonite families and that the members of the Sydney fellowship were all "first-generation Mennonite from Australia, England, New Guinea, and South Africa. . . .

"We hope we do not represent 'a defensive and ethnocentric stance,'" he wrote. "Rejoicing in our diversity, we stand as an alternative to the traditional church and offer the world a different vision of what it means to be Christian."[111]

Later in the year the *Gospel Herald* published my article about the Mennonites of Australia. I wrote of the Hursts and their vision and quoted Foppe Brouwer, a Dutch Mennonite who had migrated to Australia after World War II. Foppe predicted significant Mennonite growth in Australia within ten years. From a later perspective my article appears over enthusiastic. The Hursts lost their Australian visas, and when I last met them they were serving in the U.S. But they still hoped to be able to get back into Australia and to lead in developing an alternate way of being a church.[112]

The question of how freely to criticize when seeking to make a point and sharpen a vision remains an open one with me. We can find examples of sharp critiques in sources we consider authentic. The apostle Paul in the letter to the Galatians leaned heavily on those he perceived as trusting in works rather than grace. Menno Simons waxed eloquent at times against the practices of Roman Catholics, Zwinglians, Lutherans, and others who "make valid their positions, faith, and conduct with the sword."[113] Yet as Julia implied, a critique is easier than a strongly developed vision. But if we do have an alternative vision, how shall we enhance it?

When I returned from Australia near the end of February, I found that Alma Mater had called. Jay B. Landis, chair of the Language and Literature Department at Eastern Mennonite College invited me to teach a course called "Feature Writing" the next fall. I had been teaching Sunday school for fifty years and had led occasional workshops for writers. But to meet in a classroom for a full semester and give grades to the students would be a new experience. So I began driving nearly two hundred miles one way each week to meet my class. Feature Writing was close to what I had done as an editor, but I came into it at a different point in the process.

Traveling some four hours each way added an aspect of boredom. What should I do to occupy my mind? I found that I could connect with classical music on public broadcasting stations for most of the way. Also, I stopped occasionally to read historical markers along the road. Then I undertook a tally of churches: what denominations prevailed? I found that John Wesley's tradition led all the rest. On second thought, these were principally country churches, and I believe that Wesley's circuit writers emphasized country people.

They asked me to teach a second year and to add a course called Mass Communication. With this one I was less successful than with Feature Writing. The subject was less familiar and I worked hard to devise an adequate syllabus. At the first meeting of the class I presented this teaching plan, then called for a recess. After the recess only about half the class came back! I had expected more from them than they were prepared to put into the course.

If I could have taught this again I would have made a major revision to be more student-friendly. But about halfway through the semester one day, and about halfway home, it occurred to me that this had been a challenging experience but not a long-term priority for me. I was relieved that I was not asked again.

Instead, I signed up for classes at Pittsburgh Theological Seminary which I have described in chapter 4. This led to an opportunity to teach "Parables of Jesus" at three locations in eastern Pennsylvania. Again it called for travel, by train to Lancaster and by car to Souderton and Hinkletown. It was an interesting experience for ten weeks, but that was long enough for all that traveling.

The next year I went to Mennonite World Conference in Calcutta, India. For this conference I did not need to write a report—just go and participate. The combination of jet lag and the smog in Calcutta cut into my enjoyment, but I was glad to support the MWC. Since I had attended all but one of its assemblies since 1962, I wanted to be here also. I was impressed by the presence of 4,500 Mennonites, 3,000 of them from India. It was a well-organized and well-run meeting.

I have continued to attend the Mennonite Church General Assemblies and sit in the back with other visitors. Although I cannot see as well as in my reporting days when we had designated seating, I am impressed that assembly business sessions are open. Visitors are invited to speak if we have something to say. Occasionally I do.

It appears that in today's culture a person is not considered wise just because of advancing age. Even though, as the Preacher insisted, "There is nothing new under the sun." (Eccl. 1:9b), cultural developments are so rapid today that fresh perspectives are more welcome than what might be called mature wisdom. I see no need to mourn this. Why should we not be expected to keep up with what is going on if we want to join the conversations?

I have never quite understood the so-called division between being and doing. It strikes me as a form of Greek categorizing and not in line with our biblical tradition.

Abraham, we are told, was a man of faith, but to demonstrate it called for going somewhere. Yet there is a danger if we focus on productive activity alone. Persons whose ability is limited deserve respect as full members of the community. This is one lesson aging can teach us if we will listen. At times the message may be, "Don't just do something, sit there!" Also at one point in my life, I would have assumed that almost any problem could be solved if we have the fortitude and the patience. Further experience has taught me that some problems resist solution no matter how hard we work and pray.

As long as we Mennonites persist in seeking to be followers of the Jesus way, I think we will have something to say. In recent Bible study, I have become particularly interested in the story of Jesus. What kind of person was he? How can we who are basically conservative carry on his radical agenda? (He was more than a "little" left of center.)

I take courage from efforts to make Jesus relevant in our day. John Howard Yoder in *The Politics of Jesus* has sought to do this on a scholarly level and has pointed out that it is our calling to be faithful rather than to try to make history come out right. Lynn Miller has given us a popular summary in the words "Mennonites believe that Jesus meant what he said and that it applies to us."

Support for this turns up in interesting places. Recently I came upon a book entitled *Jesus* by a Jewish scholar named David Flusser. I found that he has dedicated the 1997 edition "to my Mennonite friends." It is reported also that he has said, "Mennonites take Jesus seriously and I do too." How shall we respond to such a statement? Boast about what good people we are that even a Jewish scholar has noticed us? A better response would be to recognize that if he knew us better he might qualify his statement. (Actually, I understand that he has. He said that we are legalistic about our view of Jesus.)

We consider it important to be disciples of Jesus. Yet some have noticed that the picture of Jesus' disciples found in the gospel of Mark is not entirely positive. When we see how slow to learn and generally fearful they appear in Mark, we may wonder whether they are adequate models. On the other hand the candor of the Markan account is refreshing in its own way and the book of Acts shows Peter and John as leaders. After Jesus' resurrection they evidently got it together.

After more than forty years, I am still called upon to help with the work of Allegheny Mennonite Conference. Occasionally I look around the circle in a meeting of Allegheny people and realize I am the oldest person in the room. But I don't mention it and no one else seems to notice. I observe, however, that conference leaders and numbers of our Allegheny pastors are the age of my sons and I am encouraged. The mantle of leadership and the living of the vision passes from one generation to another. God be praised.

Photo Album

My father with his family in 1904 when he was ten. Left to right; front: Melvin (Dad), Milford. Middle: Katherine, Levi, and Mae. Back: Truman, Ida, and Eugene.

(left) The "sharp dressers": Melvin, seated, and Milford.
(bottom left) Dad's high school senior photo.
(bottom right) Dad as a clown in 1914, when he was twenty.

(above left) My mother with her sisters. Front: Elizabeth and Alice. Back: Mayme and Susan (Mother).

(above right) Melvin with Silas Hertzler, who would later publish the Hertzler-Hartzler Family History.

My parents' 1924 wedding photo. He married a minister's daughter.

This undated photo was probably taken in 1934 and shows Katherine, Truman, Paul, and Dan. Paul died in the summer of 1934.

Dan at about age ten.   *Dan in college.*

A late 1960s family photo. Front: Dan and Mary with Dan Mark. Back: Dennis, Ronald, and Gerald

Reporting for the Periodical Division at a mid-1970s session of the Mennonite Church General Assembly.
Photo by D. Michael Hostetler. Used by permission.

The Gospel Herald editor in 1983.
Photo by Richard A. Kauffman. Used by permission of Mennonite Publishing House.

With Mary in the mid-1980s.

With my siblings in the mid-1990s: Katherine, Truman, and Martha.

With former Gospel Herald editor Paul Erb and news editor David E. Hostetler at Daniel Kauffman grave, Alverton, Pa.

Photo by Richard A. Kauffman, from *Not by Might*, copyright © 1983 by Herald Press. Used by permission of Mennonite Publishing House.

Appendix

Broken Home, Broken House?

This editorial appeared in the *Gospel Herald* on September 8, 1984. It was awarded an Associated Church Press "1984 Certificate of Recognition." The certificate was presented at the annual ACP convention in Washington, D.C., on April 15, 1985.

♦ ♦ ♦

"It takes a heap o' 'livin' in a house t' make it home." —Edgar A. Guest (1881-1959)

Mary and I took a few days vacation recently to help our third son and his wife rehabilitate an old house they bought in the spring. Apparently solid at the core, the house was showing its age at the edges (how that south side did need paint) and we labored valiantly toward restoration.

We also wondered vaguely how a house could be allowed to run down in this fashion. Didn't people care about their investment? Absentee landlords, one is given to understand, allow properties to decay because repairs cost money and it is cheaper to let them run down. But owners who live in a house are expected to keep it up.

Then we looked at the house's official records and we thought we found a clue. Although for nearly half its more than 60 years the house was owned by one family, since 1962 it has had about six different owners and half the couples divorced.

Now I have heard discussions of the effect of divorce on wives and children, for example, but I do not recall having read any study of what divorce does to houses. Clearly one house is too small a sample from which to draw firm conclusions, but the sequences in the abstracts of this one old house did impress us. As poignant as any was the case of the wife who was under age at the time of the purchase and within three years was divorced and was awarded the house. No doubt keeping the house in good repair was the last thing on her troubled mind.

None of us can fully comprehend the complex of factors pushing married people toward divorce. Surely one is the easygoing attitude in our culture toward contracts and promises. While we show mercy to those caught in a marital breakup, as we must in the name of Christ, we may at the same time support faithfulness and stability in marriage as called for by loyalty to God. We may also call attention to some of the positive side effects of good marriages, such as what they may do for houses as well as for the partners and their children.

There is doubtless no captivity quite like that of being married to an irresponsible mate. The evidence for this is documented repeatedly by letters to the answer girls syndicated in newspapers. It is illustrated also in an off-handed fashion by stories such as that of a wife in a denomination of the Anabaptist tradition who did not believe in divorce—so she poisoned her husband! Further support comes from reports that the home is the most violent sector of our society.

Yet Jesus in his sweeping defense of marital fidelity insisted that marriage vows have cosmic significance. And Paul wrote to the Corinthians that sexual intercourse is similarly binding. It is good to remind ourselves that commitments are not to be taken lightly.

It is also worthwhile noting that many resources are available today for the support of troubled marriages. Thought it may not be expected that all of these can be untangled, the word from marriage counselors is that almost nothing unsucceeds like divorce. And look what it does to houses!

The humor in the Bible is generally subtle, especially when viewed through translation. And because we take the Bible seriously, we may not expect to find jokes in it. But the writer of Jonah must surely have expected some people to chuckle over his closing lines.

As you may recall, in the last chapter of the book, Jonah is sitting outside to see what will happen to the city of Ninevah. A vine grows up to shade him and then is killed by a worm. This " useless" death of the vine makes Jonah bitter.

God chides him for the bitterness and points out that if Jonah is concerned about a plant it is appropriate for God to be concerned about a city with thousands of people, "and also much cattle" (Jon. 4:11). Surely, Jonah if you don't care about the people, at least think about all the money tied up in those cows!

So in the spirit of Jonah we might say, Beware of divorce. It's bad for your partner, it's bad for your children. And if you don't care about them, look what it does to houses! —*Daniel Hertzler*

Notes

1. *Fifty Years Building on the Warwick* (Denbigh, Va.: Warwick River Mennonite Church), 101.

2. Evelyn King Mumaw, "Susanna's Story" (Waynesboro, Va.: Jonathan D. Shenk Video, 1991). Susanna's story and related details are also offered in Mumaw's telling of her own family history (which overlaps with mine) in *The Merging: A Story of Two Families and Their Child* (Telford, Pa.: Pandora Press U.S., DreamSeeker Books, 2000).

3. *Gospel Herald*, March 26, 1914, 808.

4. Albert H. Gerberich, *The Brenneman History.* (Scottdale, Pa.: Printed by Mennonite Publishing House, 1938), 6.

5. John H. Shenk, *My Father Daniel Shenk.* (Sarasota, Fla.: Published by the author, 1995), 5, 7.

6. *Ibid.*, 9.

7. *Ibid.*, 23.

8. *Eastern Mennonite School Bulletin*, 1923-1924, p. 61. Also "Student's Record," No. 241. Her grades were as follows: Bible History, 95; Bible Geography, 96; Gospels, 88; O.T. Bk. St., 94; Latin, 95; Music II, 97.

9. The birthdays of Katherine, Truman and Martha are riveted in my mind. Paul's is from *The Hertzler-Hartzler Family History*, 629. The same source gives my mother's date of death as May 5. However her obituary in *Gospel Herald*, June 27, 1935, p. 287 gives it as May 6.

10. *Gospel Herald*, June 27, 1935, p. 287.

11. Silas Hertzler, *The Hertzler-Hartzler Family History* (Berne, Ind.: Economy Printing Concern, 1952), 11.

12. Ibid., 621.

13. *Ibid.*, 682.

14. J. Lemar and Lois Ann Mast, *As Long As Wood Grows and Water Flows.* (Morgantown, Pa., Conestoga Mennonite Church, 1982), 8, 9.

15. Paton Yoder, *Eine Wurzel: Tennessee John Stoltzfus* (Lititz, Pa.:

Sutter House, 1979).

16. *Ibid.*, 34, 50, 51, 143 (footnote 50).

17. *Ibid.*, 60.

18. Ibid., 70-72.

19. *Ibid.*, 128.

20. *Ibid.*, 127.

21. Mrs. T. K. Hershey, "A Brief History of the Congregation at Concord, Tenn." *Gospel Herald* (Nov. 24, 1953), 1121.

22. *With*, May, 1972, p.8.

23. See John A. Hostetler, *The Amish* (Herald Press, 1995) pp. 12, 20.

24. *Christian Living*, March, 1965, p. 2.

25. *Ibid.*

26. The six degrees were as follows: A.B. Eastern Mennonite College, 1951;

Th. B. Eastern Mennonite College, 1952; B.D. Goshen College Biblical Seminary, 1955; M. Ed. University of Pittsburgh, 1963; Ph. D. University of Pittsburgh, 1966; S.T.M. Pittsburgh Theological Seminary, 1995.

27. C.S. Lewis, *Surprised by Joy*. (New York: Harcourt, Brace, 1955), 137.

28. *Weather Vane*, April 22, 1966.

29. J. Lemar and Lois Ann Mast, *As Long as Wood Grows and Water Flows*, (Conestoga Mennonite Church, 1982), 58.

30. Grant M. Stoltzfus, *Mennonites of the Ohio and Eastern Conference*, (Herald Press, 1969), 201.

31. *Ibid.*, 295, 296.

32. *Ibid.*, 215, 216.

33. Masts, 96.

34. *Ibid.*, 97.

35. *Ibid.*, 98.

36. *Confession of Faith In a Mennonite Perspective* (Herald Press, 1995).

37. This Allegheny Mennonite Conference material is available in the Conference archives, at Somerset, Pennsylvania.

38. James M. Lapp, "Conferences and Congregations: A Review of Mennonite Church Polity," *Mennonite Historical Bulletin*, Vol. LVI, No. 3, July, 1995, 7.

39. Lyle E Schaller, *21 Bridges to the 21[40.] Century* (Abingdon Press, 1994), p. 29.

40. *Ibid.*, 65,66.

41. *Mennonite Encyclopedia V*, 635.

42. Paul Toews, *Mennonites In America, 1930-1970*, (Herald Press, 1996), 285, 286.

43. *Ibid.*, 340.

44. *Ibid.*, 342.

45. *Not by Might* (Herald Press, 1983), p. 168.

46. *Mennonite Yearbook and Directory, Vol. XLIV*, 1953, p. 29.

47. *Mennonite Yearbook and Directory, Vol. XLIII*, 1952, p. 28.

48. Gospel Herald, Oct. 10, 1950, p. 996.

49. *The World Book Encyclopedia* 1957, Vol. 10, pp 4483, 4484.

50. *Gospel Herald*, July 1, 1997, p. 9.

51. *Mennonite Yearbook and Directory Vol. XLVIII*, 1957, pp. 25, 26.

52. *The Mennonite Community*, Jan. 1947.

53. *Christian Living*, July 1954, p. 34.

54. *Mennonite Yearbook and Directory*, Vol. XLVIII, 1957, p. 25.

55. *Herald Adult Bible Studies*, October, November, December, 1958, pp.57, 58.

56. Thomas H. Groome, *Christian Religious Education*, (Harper & Row, 1980). See esp. chap. 10, "Shared Praxis in Praxis," pp. 207-238.

57. *Adult Bible Study Guide*, September, October, November, 1993, p. 5.

58. *Gospel Herald*, 1993, p. 15.

59. *The Jerome Biblical Commentary*, (Prentice-Hall, 1968), p. 5

60. "For the Bible tells me so," *Gospel Herald*, June 13, 1995, p. 2.

61. The 1964 issue of *Mennonite Yearbook* lists seventeen persons with editorial assignments at Mennonite Publishing House. A number of these had part-time assignments, such as for example, Helen Alderfer and Victor Stoltzfus with *Christian Living*. Of the seventeen persons only two had journalism degrees: executive editor Ellrose Zook and Willard Roth, editor of *Youth's Christian Companion*.

62. *Christian Living*, Feb. 1956, p. 4.

63. *Christian Living*, March, 1956, p. 12.

64. *Christian Living*, July, 1956, p. 29.

65. *Christian Living*, May, 1956, p. 2.

66. *Herald Adult Bible Studies*, October, November, December, 1965, pp. 3,4.

67. His obituary appears in *Gospel Herald*, August 2, 1966, p. 691.

68. *Christian Living*, January, 1964, p. 22.

69. P. 23.

70. The title of my dissertation was "Factors Related to the Comprehension of Theological Language by Mennonite Laymen." Today that title might be considered sexist. If so, it could be revised to read "laity" instead of "laymen." The point was that ordained clergy were not included in the study.

71. *1970 Annual Report*. Mennonite Publishing House, p. 14. See

Appendix A for a comparison of circulation between 1970 and 1984.

72. *1972 Annual Report*, p. 9.

73. *1973 Annual Report*, Exhibit 10; *1974 Annual Report*, Exhibit 10.

74. *1982-83 Annual Report*, p. 35.

75. *1972 Annual Report*, p. 9.

76. *Christian Living*, October, 1973, p. 32.

77. *With*, May, 1974, p. 37.

78. *1977-78 Annual Report*, p. 24.

79. *1983-84 Annual Report*, p. 33.

80. *1978-79 Annual Report*, p. 31; *1979-80 Annual Report*, pp. 31, 32; *1982-83 Annual Report*, pp. 37, 38.

81. *1978-79 Annual Report*, p. 30.

82. *1977-78 Annual Report*, p. 26.

83. *1978-79 Annual Report*, p. 30; *1979-80 Annual Report*, p. 31.

84. *1980-81 Annual Report*, p. 17.

85. *Mennonite Weekly Review*, July 9, 1981.

86. *1984-85 Annual Report*, p. 32.

87. *Auburn Views*, winter 1998, p. 5.

88. "What makes church news?", *Gospel Herald*, December 7, 1976, p. 946.

89. "Readers Say," *Gospel Herald*, February 1, 1977, p. 101.

90. "General Board Ok's sexuality document, appoints interim executive secretary," *Gospel Herald*, April 23, 1985, p. 289.

91. "Seeking the Kingdom at Eureka," August 26, 1976, p. 590. "Reflections on Assembly 75" followed on p. 592 with six authors.

92. "Our own agenda," *Gospel Herald*, March 14, 1978, p. 228.

93. "Skipping an issue," *Gospel Herald*, November 21, 1978, p. 932.

94. "GH—75-83," *Gospel Herald*, January 4, 1983, p. 16.

95. "A concern about faithfulness," *Gospel Herald*, February 17, 1987, p. 120.

96. *Gospel Herald*, October 3, 1973, p. 747.

97. From the issue of 1988-1989 to the issue of 1995, *Mennonite Yearbook* lists these three sons with these responsibilities: John A. Lapp, Executive Secretary, Mennonite Central Committee; James Lapp, Executive Secretary, Mennonite Church General Board; Joseph Lapp, President, Eastern Mennonite College.

98. The photo appears in *Gospel Herald*, September 23, 1980.

99. "Someone got the wrong number," *Gospel Herald*, January 27, 1998.

100. *Religious Education*, Vol. LXVII, No. 5, September-October, 1972, p. 413.

101. *Gospel Herald*, April 9, 1974, p. 320; August 6, 1974, p. 600; September 3, 1974, p. 657.

102. *Gospel Herald*, December 9, 1975, p. 880; December 16, 1975, p.898. "Africa Report," March 16, 1976, p. 209.

103. *Gospel Herald*, November 1, 1983, p. 768; November 15, 1983, p. 803; November 22, 1983, p. 828.

104. *Gospel Herald*, June 17, 1986, p. 428; July 1, 1986, p. 460; July 8, 1986, p. 460; July 15, 1986, p. 492.

105. *Gospel Herald*, March 6, 1990, p. 176; March 13, 1990, p. 192; March 20, 1990, p. 208.

106. *Not by Might*, Gospel Herald Sampler, (Herald Press, 1983), p. 18.

107. *Gospel Herald*, Feb. 5, 1991, p. 2.

108. *Gospel Herald*, Feb. 19,1991, p. 10.

109. *Gospel Herald*, May 7, 1991, pp. 6, 7.

110. *Gospel Herald*, June 18, 1991, pp. 4, 5.

111. *Gospel Herald*, July 30, 1991, p. 5.

112. *Gospel Herald*, November 26, 1991, pp. 5, 6, 8.

113. John C. Wenger, ed., *The Complete Writings of Menno Simons* (Scotdale, Pa.: Herald Press, 1956), p. 175.

The Author

Daniel Hertzler grew up in Berks County, Pennsylvania. As this book recounts, he was an editor at Mennonite Publishing House, Scottdale, Pennsylvania from 1952 to1990. He edited *Mennonite Community Magazine, Christian Living, Builder, Gospel Herald*, and a variety of Christian education publications.

In 1960 he was ordained to the ministry by Allegheny Mennonite Conference for his work as an editor. He has held a variety of offices in the conference, including moderator and chair of the Leadership Commission.

As described in *A Little Left of Center*, Hertzler was late to school a number of times and also late in leaving school. His last foray into higher education was undertaken after retirement, when he studied for an S.T.M. degree at Pittsburgh Theological Seminary and wrote a thesis on "The Rhetoric of the Parable of the Sower in the Gospel of Mark."

Hertzler is now an instructor for Unit II of Pastoral Studies Distance Education and an editor for Pandora Press U.S. He and his wife Mary are members of Kingview Mennonite Church, Scottdale.